VISIONARY LEADERSHIP
A Proven Pathway to Visionary Change

William A. Ihlenfeldt, Ph.D.

authorHOUSE®

AuthorHouse™
1663 Liberty Drive
Bloomington, IN 47403
www.authorhouse.com
Phone: 1-800-839-8640

© 2011 William A. Ihlenfeldt, Ph.D.. All rights reserved.

No part of this book may be reproduced, stored in a retrieval system, or transmitted by any means without the written permission of the author.

First published by AuthorHouse 1/10/2011

ISBN: 978-1-4567-2879-3 (e)
ISBN: 978-1-4567-2880-9 (dj)
ISBN: 978-1-4567-2881-6 (sc)

Library of Congress Control Number: 2011900290

Printed in the United States of America

Any people depicted in stock imagery provided by Thinkstock are models, and such images are being used for illustrative purposes only. Certain stock imagery © Thinkstock.

This book is printed on acid-free paper.

Because of the dynamic nature of the Internet, any Web addresses or links contained in this book may have changed since publication and may no longer be valid. The views expressed in this work are solely those of the author and do not necessarily reflect the views of the publisher, and the publisher hereby disclaims any responsibility for them.

Acknowledgement

The backdrop for this book is a career that I found to be exciting, challenging, and fulfilling. As I look back at that career I realize that it is a mosaic of experiences, mentors, and information. Visionary leadership, as defined in this book, is not an inherent trait, nor is it a style for which anyone can take individual credit. Rather, it is a process that is the cumulative acceptance and intertwining of the best and worst of our experiences.

By writing this book I hope that I can acknowledge and give gratitude to those who influenced me throughout my career. I include in that list the many friends, colleagues, and supervisors who probably never knew they influenced me. I also include those formal teachers to whom I owe a debt of gratitude, and, most importantly, I include the influence of my wife, Barbara, my daughters, Heidi and Holly, and my parents.

Contents

Acknowledgement v

Foreword – William H. Graves, Ph.D. ix

Introduction – The Case for Visionary Leadership and Change 1

Step One – Determining Where You Can Add Value 9
    Perception is reality.

Step Two – The Guiding Principles of Risk Taking 21
    When people tell you something is not possible, you know you are on the cutting edge.

Step Three – The Magic within your Crystal Ball—Data 33
    If you don't measure it, you can't change it.

Step Four – Making Your Vision Real—Modeling the Plan 49
    It's all about the bottom line.

Step Five – Developing an Agile Leadership Team 63
    Feed them a fish and they eat for a day; teach them how to fish and they eat for a lifetime.

Step Six – Partnerships: The Glue for Your Visionary Plan 77
    As a visionary, never worry about recognition.

Conclusion – The Personal Traits of a Visionary 93
    Everything you need to know you learned in high school.

About the Author 105

Foreword

When I first met Bill Ihlenfeldt almost a decade ago, I knew within minutes that he was a college president who put mission above position. He quickly and proudly let me know that his college, Chippewa Valley Technical College (CVTC), had the lowest per-student expenditures among its peer two-year colleges in Wisconsin. At a time when many college presidents were reluctantly increasing net tuition to students or mired down arguing the case for increasing per-student subsidies from government sources, Ihlenfeldt was energetically bringing together his colleagues and his community in a partnership effort to improve not only the quality and value of the CVTC educational experience to the student, but also the community's return on investment in the college.

The "partners" went on to increase the scale, the rate, and the economic and civic relevance of degree and certificate completions at CVTC, and did so at mutually affordable costs to its "external investors"—students, families, employers, donors, and governments. Ihlenfeldt led this effort from what SunGard Higher Education CEO Ron Lang refers to as "outside in." Ihlenfeldt knew that doing what is best for students and other external investors is not only the right thing for a college president to do, but in his context was also the surest path to increasing and sustaining community and state support for CVTC into the future.

In this book, Bill Ihlenfeldt recounts his years of experience in higher education as a means to illuminate leadership principles in action. He illustrates and formalizes the leadership principles and strategies that enabled him to convince his colleagues and his community that he, as president, would go where "they would lead him," provided that they would base their advice on documented evidence of educational need and probable outcomes. Leading by example, Ihlenfeldt created a culture of evidence at CVTC through his own professional use of performance reporting and analytics tools in conjunction with the college's student information system, its other administrative systems, and available external databases that reflected education needs. I've met no postsecondary leader more accomplished than Bill Ihlenfeldt at improving educational attainment, its affordability at scale, and its relevance in terms of measurable economic and civic impacts.

Today's policy makers recognize, as never before, that postsecondary educational attainment is the keystone in sustaining environmental, economic, and civic security into the future. Governments accordingly are not leaving the conduct of the global "brains race" for intellectual capital in the sole hands of educators. Those who hope to lead postsecondary education into the future (from inside the education enterprise) would do well to read Bill Ihlenfeldt's account of his leadership journey and, especially, to heed his organized and well illustrated advice on how **both** to talk the talk and walk the walk of a visionary leader.

William H. Graves, Ph.D.
Sr. V.P. for Academic Strategy
SunGard Higher Education

Introduction – The Case for Visionary Leadership and Change

Our country is in dire need of inspiration from leaders in all sectors who have the vision to lead our organizations in new directions, develop new products, and stimulate us to move our world toward a new horizon. If you have purchased this book, you probably believe that to be true and are in one of the following three categories: a) a new president, chief executive officer, or leadership staff; b) a person anticipating a move to a leadership position; or c) a veteran leader who is seeking new ideas. Regardless of your position, you are looking not only to lead an organization but more importantly to anticipate its future and bring the necessary changes to the organization that will make it a respected authority and an organization that is cutting new trails.

The world needs people who are excited about our future and the endless possibilities it affords. We need leaders who are willing to step forward, take charge, and lead us in directions heretofore not uncovered. This book and the process it outlines will help you to uncover and develop aspects of your leadership style that can make you the type of visionary leader that you have desired to be but have not known how to become. How many times have you been invited to a conference where the keynoter is billed as a futurist or a visionary? How many times do you hear the statement that he or she really has vision? Most leadership position postings today are calling for a person with vision, and whether it's a Fortune 500 company or a college or university, leaders are expected to see the future and lead others towards it. Don't let anxieties or self doubts stop or even hinder you; rather, be proud that you have taken the first steps to find out more about vision and visionary leadership, and you will find that your crystal ball is already within you.

You may feel that visionary leadership is not a part of your professional makeup and that because it does not seem to be in your genes you are relegated to a level of listening to others to determine the vision or future. The purpose of this book is to debunk that myth and help you to understand the concept of visionary leadership and, most importantly, become the visionary that is so critical for today's leaders, but first let me try and tell you why we need visionary leaders. Perhaps this is my chance to get on the proverbial soapbox, wax philosophical, and tell you why I really wrote this book.

I firmly believe that many sectors of our country need to change. We've all heard about change from politicians to motivational speakers, but I am talking about real change, change that takes intestinal fortitude and not just words. We need people who are willing to be creative, take risks, and stay to see the results. We saw it after World War II when the returning veterans were willing to start new business by putting their names and savings on the line to start the businesses that are considered mainstream today. As a country we've become complacent; we want to start at the top and not pay our dues. Thus we have a lot of leaders who know how to talk the talk but not walk the talk.

Down through the years I saw these individuals and even lost position advancements to them. We used to refer to them as "slow walking, fast talking." Well, in education or any other sector for that matter, we can no longer afford to walk slow and talk fast. Rome is burning, as the saying goes, and after forty years in leadership, I am concerned: concerned for our future and concerned about the future of our country in a global economy. In 2010 we are still following some of the same operating principles that were designed for an earlier era.

You might question that assertion, but think about it. For example, we still operate on an agrarian calendar in academia, a calendar that was

Introduction – The Case for Visionary Leadership and Change

developed so that farm kids could help on the farm! Why should our schools not operate year round? You can go from there to manufacturing, where we have shipped many good-paying jobs overseas because we want to create wealth by manipulating money as opposed to making things. Then let's move on to the financial institutions and our very own government. We all know how successful the leadership has been there.

Lee Iacocca recently wrote a book titled *Where Have All the Leaders Gone?* It intrigued me because I still have his first book, his autobiography, that my wife gave me in 1984. Twenty-six years later he is concerned enough about the future of this country to write another book. His latest book emphasizes the need for visionary leaders to once again bring needed innovation and creativity to our shores. Being a car enthusiast who followed the auto industry, I was, of course, interested in his first book. More importantly, I was intrigued with the creative leadership style he utilized at Ford and later as he reorganized Chrysler Corporation. Iacocca's words were poignant in 1984 when he stated, "I learned about the strength you can get from a close family life. I learned to keep going, even in bad times. I learned not to despair, even when my world was falling apart. I learned that there are no free lunches. And I learned about the value of hard work. In the end, you've got to be productive. That's what made this country great–and that's what's going to make us great again." That was in 1984, not 2010!

Those words resonated with a farm boy from Wisconsin whose father believed that fun didn't begin until the work was done and that where there is a will, there is a way. As much as I detested that philosophy during my teenage years, I always knew that he was right and that his philosophy for running a family farm on the shores of Lake Michigan was not much different from that of Lee Iacocca or from what I am defining as visionary leadership. They always say that what goes around comes around!

Another mentor of mine during the early years of my career, Stanley J. Spanbauer, speaking of education, said in his book *Quality First In*

Education…Why Not?: "Because the problem is cultural, there needs to be a different approach. The attitude to constantly improve quality and productivity must be ingrained in the very culture in which educators work. Those in command must realize that additional resources can come only when more is accomplished per educator this year than last. This can be done by applying business and industry models of quality and productivity at the very core of education." This was written in 1987. Here we are in 2010, and those same words ring true today! How much true change has occurred in the last twenty-five years—or even in the last forty-five years?

Both of these examples point out why we need visionary leaders who can both walk the walk and talk the talk, and we need them now more than ever! I don't want to be so brash as to say that there are no visionary leaders, but you and I both know they are few and far between. Too many times we want to be visionary by saying words that were spoken decades before, words that may inspire us. But words alone won't create the new world we need. That takes visionary leadership!

Visionary leadership carries with it a hefty price tag. It carries that price tag because much of the responsibility falls on you as a senior leader. This is not a leadership scenario where you can delegate responsibility and go play golf! If you look at the successful small businesses, you will notice that they have one thing in common—an involved and committed chief executive officer. That is what it takes for visionary leadership! Surrounding yourself with the right people and delegating responsibility and all of the other attributes that we have learned in Leadership 101 are still critical, but the visionary leader is always there, always involved and selling the organization. To become a visionary leader, you need to love what you do. If you can't say that about your role, then maybe you are not cut out for this track.

That may seem harsh, but I've seen too many leaders who are in the position because that is the thing to do, not because they believe in what they are doing. After forty years in leadership roles, I can honestly say that I enjoyed every moment. Yes, there were days that I would rather

Introduction – The Case for Visionary Leadership and Change

not have faced because of one problem or another; but overall I was there because I believed I could make a difference, and I thoroughly enjoyed my role!

I have seen great practitioners move into leadership because of the money or because they were seeking upward mobility. In the final analysis they made poor leaders because their heart was not in it. As a visionary leader you need to be both visible and accessible to your staff and to your customers, and if you are not in the role because you want to be, that can lead to some tiresome days and ultimately to your demise. I remember well a mistake I made by promoting an excellent teacher into a leadership role even though my instincts told me not to. He wanted the position and had been an excellent instructor and leader in that arena. Unfortunately, his heart was in instruction, and leadership was not where he wanted to be. He retired from the organization somewhat disappointed in what had been an otherwise brilliant career. Two lessons can be learned from this. One is to trust your "gut" level intuition, and the other is to make certain that leadership is the role you really want.

Now that I've discussed the need for visionary leadership, you're probably asking yourself if this is really for you. I believe that is a fair question, one that each of us has asked at some point in our career. Let me try and give you a feeling for leadership at this level. I was involved in higher education for forty-two years in many different roles at two different colleges. Forty of those years were in some type of leadership role, and for much of that time I agonized with the idea of futuristic vision. The last fourteen years of my career afforded me the opportunity to be the president of a seven-campus technical college serving 20,000 students annually. Of course, when you step into that role, "the vision thing" becomes especially critical. Everyone wants—even expects—you to have a vision and to be able to articulate it clearly. If you look at the selection process for presidents in the higher education, you will see what I mean. As I look back at my experience, I recall that at the time I questioned the need for much of the process; but in retrospect I can see it was intended to look at my background and thinking in relation to where the college was and where the trustees felt it needed to go. The process included community sessions, sessions with staff, social situations, and of course the traditional interview situation with the trustees. They were looking to understand my vision for the college and whether that fit with their thinking. I am not sure that any of us understood the task in front of us at that time, but the extensive process was designed to give them a snapshot of my leadership capability and vision and to validate what I was saying. This book utilizes my experiences as college president to lead you through the process of becoming the visionary leader in a way you may not have thought possible.

I am here to tell you that many individuals in top leadership roles don't have a clue as to what visionary leadership is or should be, and thus they have compromised their ability to be top-notch leaders or change agents for their organizations. In fact, they have become caretakers for their organizations rather than the leaders that their co-workers expect. This world can no longer afford caretakers in leadership roles; rather, we need people with inspiration and vision.

Now don't get me wrong. These individuals develop strategic plans, vision statements, missions, and goals that they create by consensus and use to move their organizations forward. So I am not saying that these individuals are poor leaders. Nevertheless, they never quite achieve the level of competence that causes people to look to them for that glimpse into the future, nor do they create the type of organization, products, or service that stand out among others.

We are not going to be talking about a vision statement that most organizations put together by consensus as part of their strategic planning or environmental scanning processes. Rather, we will be discussing that seemingly innate capability that some leaders seem to have which allows them to anticipate the future and lead others in that direction before the path can be clearly seen. These are the unique individuals who help us to see the world in a different way or light. Down through the years our world has been influenced by these unique visionary leaders. Individuals like Edwards Deming, Franklin Roosevelt, Ronald Reagan, John Kennedy,

Introduction – The Case for Visionary Leadership and Change

Steven Spielberg, Lee Iacocca and renowned leaders in many professions and leadership roles seemed to enjoy an insight into what was necessary for us to succeed in the future and were able to convince others that they were right! These individuals were visionary leaders, and even today they are recognized as such.

In this book I will attempt to dissect this thing called "visionary leadership" and put it in a perspective that will help you to evolve into a "visionary" leader. I will utilize my forty-two year technical college career as a basis that will make it especially meaningful to the higher education community. Visionary leadership became a passion of mine early in my presidency when in the exit interview with an accrediting body for the college, the chair, who was a fellow president, gave me the advice that he was able to be a president for twenty-eight years because he waited until others on the staff brought forward ideas to move his organization forward, and then he would help support those issues. That statement has stayed with me to this day! I remember thinking to myself, "If this is what leadership is all about, then I am in the wrong career."

When I first became a college president, I knew I had inherited a college that needed to change direction quite rapidly if it was to get on track and become competitive in the current evolving market. The college's financial situation was not good. Operational reserves were at minimal levels, and access to resources from the federal, state, and local level was dwindling. Similarly, the college had experienced declining enrollments for the past years, and in higher education, student enrollments equate to the production output of a business. This was not a pretty picture for a college or a business. I was also aware that the internal climate was good. People liked the way things were going. There had been little change over the past decade, and the pace was comfortable. Education in the early '90s was a secure place to be employed, with little or no threat of job loss.

They say it is lonely at the top, and I began to understand what it meant. I could project finances into the future, and the balance sheet did not look good. Yet staff did not see the same need to be concerned.

In fact, most of them weren't even aware of the financial picture of the college; even worse, many didn't care. That was the responsibility of someone else, and their only task was to submit information for budget preparation once a year and then complain if they didn't get everything they asked for.

Strategic planning did take place annually, but in many ways it was an exercise more than an integral process. The process was mainly internal with little if any external participation. Government-generated data was presented, and a large document was produced which was not focused and which allowed anybody to do anything. Although the large document was impressive, it commonly ended up on the shelf and everybody went on doing what they always did. Now this assessment may seem negative, but I believe it is typical of a lot of organizations and businesses, and it is certainly does not exemplify visionary leadership! So let's begin and give you the rest of the story!

We will begin by taking a critical look at this thing we call vision and determine the steps that can help leaders to be more effective. The six steps to becoming a visionary leader that will be discussed are as follows:

- defining your value
- developing personal parameters for risk analysis
- using data and forecasting models
- modeling the plan
- developing a leadership team
- forming partnerships

I will also utilize some case studies to give you a blow-by-blow description of visionary leadership, showing you how to utilize these steps as you develop the crystal ball within you.

Step One – Determining Where You Can Add Value

Perception is reality.

It is my contention that there is nothing mystical or innate about visionary leadership. Rather, leaders who are considered visionary are individuals who apply the six steps outlined in this book in a consistent and cohesive manner. Individuals do not become visionaries right out of the chute. By being consistent over time, they developed the image of one who is able to anticipate or, more importantly, create the future. Consistency is the key word. Developing a solid plan and sticking to that plan with consistency is the necessary foundation for visionary leadership. I know that staff who worked with me would often think, "There he goes again! We've heard that information more times than we care to think about." But without consistency in plan you have chaos. As the saying goes, develop a plan that is solid and then stick to it and talk about it every chance you have. I developed handouts, power point presentations, and newsletters for internal and external groups that outlined my plans, and I never missed an opportunity to use them! Wherever and whenever people were willing to listen, I was ready and prepared to tell the story.

If you study the backgrounds of visionary leaders, you will also find that a common thread among them is that they have carefully studied others and have utilized them almost in quasi-mentoring roles. These leaders have an uncanny ability to glean from the best and use these skills to their benefit to add value for others. As I look back at my career, I can identify a half-dozen people from whom I gained extremely valuable expertise. While I am not like any one of them, I have utilized leadership traits from each of them to further my career. I know that without those learning experiences I would not have enjoyed the career that I did. I even found myself thinking at various times during my career that I did not like the way a certain person led at the time; but looking back, I find that I injected certain aspects of that person's leadership into my own style.

You are probably beginning to realize that a lot of visionary leadership has to do with the perception that others have of your leadership style, and that is right on! In fact, visionary leadership has much to do with the perceived value of the leader to the organization and to its members. I will emphasize that it is more than just perceived value; it is truly perceived *added value*; and it is that perceived *added value* that you will learn to bring to your organization that is at the very heart of visionary leadership. Your perceived value as a leader is achieved over time by the creativity and innovation you bring to the organization that the staff feels would not have been possible or at least not as possible without you. The perception that others have of you is developed over time, and it is very fragile; thus consistency and the ability to glean strategies from the successes of others are key elements.

If you are going to be perceived as adding value to your organization, then you really need to begin by getting down to the traditional "who, what, and why" questions of the organization you are leading. You need to determine who needs to view you as providing value for them, what they perceive as needing attention, and, in the broadest sense, what they will perceive as being of added value to them? Of course, the most important point is determining why it is of value to them, because that is what will usually lead you to a visionary solution. It is important not to make the critical error of believing that leadership is simply giving people what they are asking for. That is not leadership in any sense of the word; it is certainly not visionary leadership. You will be paid to determine the value-added direction for your organization, and that means you are responsible for separating fact from fiction. The solution that adds value may be the one people are asking for, or it may be totally different. That is for you to determine, and that is visionary leadership. So beyond consistency of purpose and learning from others, how do we determine the value-added solutions and get that glimpse of the future toward which others will follow?

From my earliest days in leadership I have always benefited from my psychology education, and in fact I believe that many of the premises of psychological counseling can be of benefit to leaders. You will find me referring to these premises at various times in this book, for I believe they are utilized by visionary leaders in forming a foundation for their work and answering the "who, what, and why" questions that ultimately lead to adding value for the customers and the organization.

The first of these premises and perhaps the most important one to internalize is introspection, the ability to look objectively at yourself and analyze the impact of your actions on others. In other words, you need to see yourself as others see you. If you do not do this, or are unwilling to do it, you cannot be successful. Introspection is an important key to answering the "who, what, and why" questions. It is not as easy to do as you might think, because it cannot be done in a vacuum and it must be objective. The absolute worst thing you can do is to look at yourself through rose-colored glasses, and for most of us that is difficult because it means we have to check our big egos at the door! I remember some key advice from one of my many mentors was the statement, "Well, you're a president now, but just remember, you can't act like one." That may sound like strange advice to a new leader, but it emphasizes the need for introspection and the need to derive your value from the perceptions of others. What it points out is that egos have no place in visionary leadership. Not realizing that has led to the early demise of many who came to the job with a lot of talent. It is all too easy to get caught up in the congratulatory rhetoric that goes along with a new position. My advice is to savor the moment and then get to work.

Effective introspection actually relies on two other counseling tools. Those tools are listening and observing nonverbal communication, and both can be very difficult to utilize effectively. How many times have you seen a speaker overstay their welcome when audience is tiring of them and they don't recognize the obvious feedback? Or how many times have you seen someone listen with their ears but not their brain? Have you ever felt that what you had to say was so important that you ignored time and the interest of your audience? All of these are examples of not using introspection, listening, and observation to determine value.

If you are going to answer the "who, what, and why" questions correctly, you will need to practice all of these techniques, and you will need to ask for feedback from others because it is your audience, not you, that determines what you need to know and how effectively you are in gathering that data. While this may not sound visionary, you are in fact building the foundation for the elements that will be outlined in the next steps. Observe the gleam in their eyes, the fidgeting lack of interest, or the occasional smirk that signifies rejection. Ponder the bright spots that seem to turn people on—you can and you need to learn to recognize the signs. Ask for feedback. Can they articulate the answer to your questions? Are they willing to criticize or offer alternatives to questions or positions? Open yourself up by restating their position or by articulating criticisms. This will allow you to enter their world, which, by the way, will be both intimidating and fragile. It will be intimidating because you are making yourself vulnerable to attack, and while you may be tempted to perceive vulnerability as weakness, it is the avenue to gaining trust and respect. Gaining trust is difficult, and it will be fragile, for it is easy to lose by one misspoken word. All of this formulates the perception others have of you as a leader and begins to form the relationship that is so critical to visionary leadership.

As an example of utilizing introspection, I would regularly hold open forum sessions with my staff. While these sessions were intimidating at first, I began to be comfortable with them. Later, as time went on, I was able to use them effectively to gather information. The sessions were designed to be informal, and no question or concern was off limits. I always needed to be prepared to be "hit" with those hard, uncomfortable questions by some staff; but these questions, other than a few designed to be the "gotcha" type, reflected the mood of many who were too embarrassed or unwilling to confront me with the reality of the situation. These were the questions and concerns that really got to the heart of the matter. It is easy to avoid these types of situations and to walk through the day feeling that all is well; but unless you are willing to internalize these questions and concerns in relation to yourself, you will never really understand true environment and climate that you are dealing with, and you will never utilize the power of introspection.

I would also regularly manage by "walking around," making sure to stop in and talk with my harshest critics. If you do not do this, you will never get the true pulse of your organization, and you will be living with a false sense of security. This was not always comfortable, but I recalled the words of Winston Churchill when he said, "If you are going through hell, keep going." I followed his words of wisdom, and I found that my critics would always give me a true look at how people felt about me and how things were going. It included the good, the bad, and the ugly, but at least I knew and could deal with it. In the final analysis, this approach improved staff's perception of me; and if you use introspection properly, the same will happen for you. Once you become comfortable with introspection, you are ready to answer the difficult questions surrounding value.

The first step in creating vision is to define the problem or what is lacking in an organization. Don't allow yourself to fall into that familiar trap of looking only to those that agree with your current thoughts or, as we discussed earlier, trying to deliver the proverbial wish list. True value comes from helping others solve problems important to them, not from forcing unrelated ideas on them or going with the status quo. Remember the rule: vision and value go hand in hand and are determined by others, not you!

You must learn to understand what creates value for an audience by gauging their reaction to your remarks. Now, these people will not tell you their vision of the future, but rather you will be able to determine quite readily what is not right with their world from their remarks.

Remember, visionary leaders are valuable because they create a picture of the future that is different and better than what is currently being experienced. Visions grow from problems, and visionaries are the ones who use their skills to determine which problems are important and who lead others forward in new directions.

Now, a nod of the head or a gleam in a few eyes does not determine the future, but as a visionary leader you will need to "track" these responses to determine trends that turn people on and help you identify what they perceive as important. Sound boring or mundane? Don't take it lightly, because it is the basis for the future. We all know how many people have made money in the stock market or other investments by utilizing "tips." I have also had veteran legislators tell me that their direction on policies comes many times from limited comments from key sources.

I advise you not go into this with the expectation that everyone will agree with you all of the time; rather, you need to be a leader who tracks the impact of your ideas on multiple audiences over time to determine what is valuable to them. It is not the quantity of responses, but the consistency of responses that will help you to determine true value. If you have truly listened, discussed your ideas with a variety of audiences, and searched for common agreement among them, then your sample size will not matter.

Let me relate several instances in my career when I believe I determined and added value for the customers of my organization. One of them was early on in my presidency, and one was near the end. The first involved facilities at the college that in my estimation were out of date because little new development had occurred in the past twenty years. The faculty had often talked of new facilities, but because of the necessity to do a referendum in eleven counties, the idea was dismissed because of perceived difficulty. This was one of those data elements that I stored for future use. The college's full-time equivalent numbers, which I equate to production, were decreasing, and some of the information I received from prospective and current students led me to believe they viewed our programs as being out of date not because of the curriculum, staff, or equipment but because of crowded, dated, and somewhat unsafe facilities.

Three educational areas in particular came to the forefront, and they included manufacturing facilities, emergency services facilities, and new campus facilities in the fastest-growing region of the college's district. I began to collect information formally and informally on these three areas, including growth (production) potential for the college, and found that student growth could be quite substantial if we could provide the right training at the right times and in the right numbers. Interestingly enough, the industries and agencies that utilized the graduates supported the idea and indicated that the growth in the number of our graduates would be a positive for them.

This was enough information for me to carry the thought process to the next level, so I began to engage faculty, industries and agencies in a development process. Not surprising, the ideas surfaced quite easily, and we were able to put together a series of white papers on the projects. But reading my audiences, I knew that many believed this to be a great process but one that would go nowhere. As a visionary leader, you cannot let that happen! If the idea is good and well researched, and if there seems to be customer support, you need to move it forward.

The white paper was followed by modeling of projected revenues and production (student) numbers to ensure that the thinking was grounded. Our modeling took on a new flavor in that we looked at the total operation of the college and the short- and long-term impacts of the projects. This meant dealing only with student production and corresponding operational costs and not with the facility costs, which would be dealt with another day. Too many times projects are looked at in a vacuum or on a short-term basis, a limited perspective that can create problems later on. I wanted a modeling process that was real and not based on "off the cuff numbers," as is done many times. In this process we looked at everything, including closing less productive programs and reallocating the corresponding money.

In the final analysis, the projects were deemed feasible. They would give the college growth for at least five years, and they could be done with a modest increase in revenue, some revenue coming from increased tuition, some from contracting services, and some from a small operational tax increase. Only one obstacle remained, an obstacle that had always stood in the way previously: the need for a district-wide referendum that no one thought could be done. I have always felt that I have answered the value question and have moved to the cutting edge when others tell me that my vision is good but not possible. It is at that point that you will earn your pay because others not so visionary will cash in their chips and sit back to watch you fail. Don't be deterred!

Once you have determined value for your customers, they tend to become your advocates, and that makes your job a lot easier. First of all, you have the data to communicate effectively as a visionary leader, and you are able to answer the difficult questions with ease. In this case, I found that the industries, the economic development organizations, and the unions all came to be supporters. In fact, the city and economic development organization donated ten acres of land worth thirty thousand dollars per acre in an industrial park to persuade the college to build the manufacturing center in that park rather than on the traditional campus. Furthermore, they persuaded the trustees to expand the footprint of the center, and they agreed to raise the additional money to make it happen! Perceptions had begun to change!

Communication is a key, and I personally made over 125 speeches to groups in eleven counties about the projects. This leads me to another important characteristic of visionary leaders. As a visionary leader you become the point person that people want to hear. Yes, others can help you, but as the visionary leader you will need to bear the brunt of selling your vision.

The result was that the college passed its first and only referendum in all counties with 68 percent of the vote. One year later we cut the ribbons on three new facilities. Did they add value? Yes, they did, because enrollments in each of the areas increased substantially; and because we now looked like our counterparts in industry, students were able to learn in surroundings that looked like the environments they would eventually work in. We also found increased interest from parents who encouraged their children to tour our facilities and enroll in our programs. These three facilities were a foundation that added value to the college, to its customers, to the industries they support, and to the instructors who create and teach the curriculum. Truly, it became a win-win situation that eventually allowed the college to become one of the fastest-growing colleges for its size in the nation. Perceptions began to change, not because staff had received something they wanted, but because new directions not previously considered or attempted were now possible.

The second example occurred much later in my presidency and took a lot more political capital. By "political capital" I mean the good will and positive image that leaders build over the years. The college I was at was a technical college, as are most in Wisconsin, but over the years transfer to senior universities had become a major goal of our students, as it is at most community colleges in other states. Wisconsin also has a system of two-year liberal studies colleges which are a part of the University of Wisconsin system and which allow direct or complete transfer. Such a college did not exist in the eleven counties that my college served, so our students had to choose either a technical college or a four-year university. Although transfer between the technical colleges and four-year universities had become easier over the years because of articulated agreements at the regional level, transfer was not complete, and students would always express concern that transfer of credit was important to them and remained a problem in their mind.

I recognized that "value added" was interpreted by our students as being able to start at a technical college and transfer at the end of two years without losing credits. This was not as easy as it would seem, because courses in a technical associate degree don't always align with credits in a liberal studies program. As a result, the students, to their dismay, often came out on the short end.

I began to investigate the possibility of adding a liberal studies degree to our curriculum, which would in effect make the college a community college. Three other colleges had been given that status by statute in the early 1970s because of their size and location. Since that time, however, expanding the mission of other colleges had not been allowed. The data I collected certainly supported the idea, because students in a region of one hundred square miles and more were not given the same access to higher education that students in other areas of the state and country enjoyed; and while they had access to universities in the region, enrollment caps and program schedules kept large numbers of place-bound and working students from participating. Other drawbacks included more time and higher costs for students who did transfer because they were forced to take additional credits to cover those credits that did not transfer. This practice had gone on for over twenty years!

There was no question in my mind that this was a problem that needed solving and would be a value-added proposition. Year after year, no matter how good we made the transfer process, the same problem was brought forward by community groups and student groups, indicating that we had not added value to the situation.

Believing that the idea of a liberal studies degree made sense, I put together publications and news releases on the topic outlining the need; but when the idea reached beyond my college trustees who embraced the idea, it began to hit roadblock after roadblock. At first I could not even get permission to submit a program proposal because the mission was capped, or so I was told. I was told that even if I could get it through the technical college state board, the university board of regents would never allow it. This was even before anyone was willing to review the data I had put together. Now it was my turn to be a risk taker or to sit back and accept the status quo.

I discussed political capital, which is what you need to build up as a visionary leader. The day will come when you need extraordinary support to make things happen, and I was at that point. Everything we will discuss in future steps in this book came into play, including risk taking, public relations, data and information utilization, business planning and modeling, and staff training. All were necessary if I was

Step One – Determining Where You Can Add Value

to add value for our customers. Why, you might ask, was this necessary if it was obviously a "value-added" proposition? Many times you will walk the line between a future trend and what I refer to as the "because we've always done it this way syndrome," and the latter is often the most difficult for any visionary leader to overcome. It is very powerful because it is the easiest route to take, the one that doesn't make waves, and that is what I was up against.

My proposal was reviewed in many arenas, more than I had ever expected, and it probably would have been summarily dismissed if I had not built up credibility over many years. Most knew I had done my homework. As a visionary leader, you can never move forward with a risky venture without being thoroughly prepared. You will be tested, and if you are unprepared you will be out on the proverbial limb. Always remember that just because you believe in an idea and have done your research, others may not have the same viewpoint.

Because of the political ramifications, I was required to test this proposal at the highest levels. I had to appear before a legislative taskforce that I was part of and also in front of legislative higher education committees. Fortunately, I found support among some legislators and was able to get strong student and alumni support for the proposal, which most found hard to dispute. In fact, the testimony of students in the media and in front of legislative committees was critical to the final success of the project.

After many months I was able to convince the state board of the technical colleges to hear the proposal and act on it, which they did. Technical college system approval moved the proposal to the board of regents of the university system for consideration because of the split jurisdictions in Wisconsin. Regents' approval eventually came, and finally our students were able to enjoy the transfer benefits that were missing to that point. Value added! Perceptions changed!

While these two situations are totally different in terms scope, degree of difficulty, and risk, they both exemplify the point of this chapter that value needs to be determined by the customers you are serving and not by you as a leader. Without the "value-added" potential of these projects, neither would have succeeded in the long run. Both also utilized the other steps of visionary leadership that we will discuss in future chapters, building on the premise that visionary leadership is not some innate capability that the person possesses but rather is the culmination of a well-executed process that is followed with persistence and consistency.

These two examples may not sound particularly visionary, or for that matter even exciting, and that is because beauty is in the eye of the beholder. The referendum example may sound mundane in some areas that aren't confronted with the complexity of the situation I outlined. Similarly, the transfer situation may not rise to the visionary level in states where community colleges are models of educational delivery. This exemplifies the fact that your customers are the keys. If they feel it is important and if you are able to deliver the goods, then you will have succeeded in their eyes; and over time the cumulative effect of such decisions will lead to what I am referring to as visionary leadership. You will have taken them in new directions that were never before utilized, thought of, or thought to be possible.

I will be building on these examples and many more as we proceed through the book, but remember, they all follow the same process, and that is what visionary leadership is about. It is not about giving away the store; rather, it is about charting new directions to solve existing problems within the resources at hand, and leading others by showing them the excitement of change that is possible. Perception is reality, and visionary leadership changes perceptions by adding value.

Step Two –
The Guiding Principles of Risk Taking

*When people tell you something is not possible,
you know you are on the cutting edge.*

Risk is a topic that has received a lot of attention and a lot of ink over time. Most leaders like to profess that they encourage their staff to take risks and step outside of the box, but in reality few do. In all honesty, most leaders or managers fear risk even though they publicly embrace it. Many times the fear of being wrong outweighs the desire to lead in the right direction; and the farther down the chain of command, the earlier the leader is in his or her career, and the younger he or she is the more this phenomenon is present. Leaders worry about their careers; they worry about boards of directors; they worry about people in organizations who spend their time waiting to pounce on others who are wrong, and the list goes on and on. In fact, the reasons for not taking risks seem on the surface to be greater than the reasons to encourage one to take risks.

The scenario many times becomes one of risk survival rather than one of leading with vision. How many times have we heard the term "calculated risks" or "out-of-the-box thinking," and how many times are these announced by non-visionary leaders, and yet how many times are creative individuals put down when they take the terms at face value and move forward? I had staff in my own organization tell me that new ideas never saw the light of day because someone in long chains of command stopped the ideas before they got to the top! Believe it or not, there are people in organizations who stifle out-of-the-box thinking simply because it might cause them more work!

Why, then, would you even want to consider taking risks for your organization? The answer is simple: we need to ensure that innovation, creativity, and enterprise remain the backbone of our economy and our country. Because of complacency, we have seen a decline in these core elements over the years. Look at what happened after World War II when people came back to this country and were visionary and creative enough to establish the many businesses and industries and economic growth that we now all enjoy. Since then, we as a country have become complacent, resting on our laurels and enjoying the fruits of the past. Well, it is time to regain that type of thinking and those same attitudes if we want to maintain or regain our status in this global economy. We need the innovative spirit of returning veteran; we need to believe in ourselves; we need to develop new ideas, processes, and products; we need visionary leaders to regain what we have lost in the global market place.

When, then, is risk appropriate for a visionary leader? I am going to answer that question a bit differently, utilizing the previously enumerated elements of visionary leadership. We know that value is determined by your audience or customers and that trends over time are critical even though the information at any given time might be minimal. We also know that data support is a key. Now let's apply those concepts to risk. Let's assume that, as a visionary leader, you have determined that a project or a solution would be valuable to your audience or customers over time. Now it is up to you to lead them outside of the box and convince them that what you are proposing will be a valuable solution.

As a visionary leader, you need to become comfortable with the risk involved with the projects you undertake. To accomplish your objective, you must first accept the fact that taking risks is not for the faint of heart, because risks can lead to failure. Just look at the number of successful entrepreneurs who failed before they succeeded! The high percentage will surprise you. It points to the fact that if a vision has no risk, you are

Step Two – The Guiding Principles of Risk Taking

probably following rather than leading. It also means that you can never take risk lightly.

Today, however, many leaders are afraid to step out of the box and seek the change that we want and need. The turmoil in Washington and in state capitols throughout this nation is a good example of that. Politicians have told me and others privately that they must follow the "party line" or risk losing party support or valued chair positions. This practice certainly does not speak to the development of visionary leaders in the political circles, and it becomes clear as to the reason for a lack of change in our country.

Many times leaders are afraid to take risks because they have been taught that it is important to achieve consensus to be successful. I learned quite quickly in my first college budget sessions that consensus is important but that the level at which it occurs is critical. In my case, staff wanted to be involved in shaping the budget and wanted their opinions to be heard because teams, consensus, and involvement in decisions were high on the list of needs expressed when they selected a new president. I knew the quality movement, had read the books, and even had the training, so I was resolved from the start to involve the staff and change the notion of the "good old boys in the board room making the decisions." Everybody was elated and everything worked–that is, until the hard decisions like staff reduction had to be made! Then it was I–the one earning the "big bucks"–who was expected to determine the level of risk. I'm even sure there were some who wanted to see the new president crash and burn!

I learned from that experience that staff, despite their cries for involvement and consensus building, expect their leaders to set the risk parameters. It is going to be up to you as a leader to set the stage and determine the direction. Then, within those parameters, consensus and involvement come into play. Visionary leaders must be willing to take the risks by setting that critical direction and those key parameters.

I like to approach risk using financial modeling. In this case modeling showed clearly that the college was facing a financial crisis that would require serious change to turn around. The algorithms used in modeling are "if-then" statements that I develop to model various ideas. They may not give me the total answer, but they force me to look at things objectively. An example of a simple algorithm would be, "If the student population increases by a given amount, then the cost of operations will increase by a consistent amount." Obviously, linear projections have shortcomings, but for modeling purposes they provide consistency and objectivity.

In the example above, the magnitude of change projected by the model was definitely risky. I had researched and gleaned information from the environmental scan that the trustees collected when doing the presidential search. By analyzing and synthesizing that information, I could see that the customers of the college wanted more accountability. Thus the seed for a new financial plan was sown.

As I began to collect data and do research for a new financial model for the organization, I looked to the business world for direction because education is a business– a big business. I was keenly aware that the implementation of a business-based model could fail if it was not accepted by educational faculty who felt differently about the way a college operated. Unfortunately, most educators have not been educated in business principles, and many are of the opinion that education does not, cannot, and should not operate as a business. However, there were too many elements in a business-based financial model that made sense for me to ignore it. True, the college was not used to operating that way; but these were different times and our customers–the taxpayers and the students–needed more of the services we provided even though the resources were not available.

The resulting business-based model we devised was one that was both easy to understand and measureable. Most importantly, it met our customers' expectations. That plan included five measureable elements that could transcend time:
- Increase/maintain budget reserve for emergencies/cash flow
- Reduce costs by improving processes

Step Two – The Guiding Principles of Risk Taking

- Increase enrollments in industry-demanded programs
- Reduce expenses below available resources
- Develop a long-range capital plan

All of these elements make simple sense if we are considering our personal budgets, but organizations, especially public organizations, are not used to thinking that way! For example, if resources are available, the tendency is to utilize them according to plans that many times are very broad and not based on need. Similarly, programs seem to continue on regardless of the need for graduates, thus taking resources that might be used for a program with a more pressing need; reserves for emergencies tend to be used as "slush funds" rather than for the intended use. The idea of reallocation is also somewhat foreign to public organizations, although it has become more frequent as a result of the recent downturn. All too often, reallocations are done with no real basis in need or fact. Too many times they are based on the impact or pain that the public will feel in hopes of an outcry which will save the status quo.

Many sleepless nights followed as I proceeded with development of the concept and the resulting risk, but I decided to take my case to the public. In order to minimize the risk, I called together a group of successful chief executive officers from private-sector businesses in the region and asked them to advise me. They agreed on the condition that I would call them together only when I needed them and that I would simply outline the problem and listen to their ideas. This strategy was extremely successful. It gave me ideas and insights, and it gave my ideas exposure to the public. Could failure still occur? Yes, but the risk was nowhere near as great. Remember, I stated earlier that most visionary leaders have quasi-mentors that they emulate. This is a concrete example of mentorship. Staff realized that public support, especially at that high level, gave credibility to my risk-taking.

Now you may wonder how all of this will help you determine how much risk is too much risk and how much is good visionary leadership? This is something which you have to determine based on your personal tolerance for risk, but there are several questions that you can ask yourself that can make your decision easier. First of all, do you believe the solution will work? Each decision must be well thought out to ensure beyond a reasonable doubt that the solution will in fact add value to your customers and solve their problem. If you don't personally believe that it will work, and if you don't believe in the reasoning behind it, then it is probably too risky! Remember, you will be the one on the line for this vision.

Secondly, have you done your homework? Before taking risks, you must do your homework and research, making certain that you know the subject like the back of your hand. Why do I say this? Leaders must have confidence in themselves and in their ideas, and they must be capable of exuding that confidence to their audiences. A vision is not an idea that you think up and run with. Remember, we are not politicians but rather individuals who need to be successful in order to help our organizations and others to succeed. Listening, reading, and watching are the ways that research occurs. If you cannot sell the idea, no matter how good it is, to others because you have not done the requisite preparation, then the vision is too risky.

Third, are there parts of the solution that already have been proven or tested? Visions usually involve applying a known solution to an area with which it is not normally associated. Using a business-based model in public education is such an example. It might be considered visionary by some, but then consider that educators have said for years that their discipline is different and that it has to be that way. Yet as a college president I was able to successfully apply the same business principles to the operation of a college. Programs became production units producing graduates, and a cost was applied to each unit of production at various levels. Programs that could not attract, retain, or place students in jobs were modified, put on a watch list, and ultimately suspended if expectations were not achieved. We attempted successfully to lower costs while increasing production, and for many years we were able to move the college to the lowest cost per full-time student among all of the colleges in Wisconsin, an achievement we both sought and were proud of. We were proud because during that same time we increased production significantly and maintained quality levels of both our students and our graduates. Strategic plans emphasized these goals and were tied to the final annual budget. Adaptations were made if our modeling and measurements dictated the need for modifications. Sounds like a business to me, and the principles of a business-based model can work! The point remains that this was simply an application of a known concept to an area with which it is not normally associated.

Another example from my experiences involved advanced technologies. I will discuss this in detail in Chapter Six but will use it as an example here. Manufacturing was in a decline in our state for many reasons. At the governor's request, the colleges convened executives from industries around the state to analyze the problem, develop solutions, and determine if the state's educational organizations could help to reverse this trend. The output from the session resulted in several potential solutions, but one of them stood out with special clarity. The idea involved helping existing industries to be more productive by helping them to utilize advanced technologies to develop new products and improve their processes.

That seemingly simple solution was in reality mind boggling. First we had to define advanced technology, then select appropriate trends, and finally decide how to implement. I was attending a conference later that year and had the opportunity to listen to an address on nanotechnology, a topic I was vaguely familiar with and one more commonly associated with large research universities than with two-year community and technical colleges.

But what I heard hit home. It made sense! A nearby metropolitan area was heavily invested in three major industry groupings—medical device, biotechnology, and chemical products—all of them using nanotechnology. Why not connect the dots and apply existing ideas to a different arena and train technicians to work in these industries? At the same time we could develop an applied research center to allow local industries to investigate, learn, and develop new processes and products.

I knew that I had an idea, albeit a risky idea, but how was I to determine its value? I began to talk about it. I discussed it in staff meetings, incorporated it in speeches, and discussed it with the public and wherever people were willing to listen. At the same time I was listening and gauging their reactions. Was this valuable to them? Soon nanotechnology was being discussed by others, and within a year the first nanoscience technology program was born. A year later, NanoRite, an applied research and innovation center complete with a Class 100 clean room opened. All of this at a two-year college!

Again existing knowledge was applied to a new arena, thus reducing the risk for part of the equation. A risk was taken, a risk considered visionary by some; but in reality it was the result of a series of very calculated steps involving research, determining value to others, setting parameters, and then moving forward, always continuing that research and measurement of progress.

You may have noticed that both of these examples happened within a very short period of time. That brings up the important fourth question: Are you and your organization capable of responding quickly when necessary? Speed-to-market is based on the quality of the systems you have in place to deal with emerging problems. If these rapid-response systems are not in place, you probably are not ready to take the risk. Too many times in organizations, we talk things to death and never act. If you are going to be a visionary leader worth your salt, speed-to-market needs to become a part of your vocabulary and thus a part of your systems. You cannot discuss things while Rome burns; rather, you must be prepared to proceed as rapidly as your risk tolerance and research allows you. Thus your research systems need to be capable of analyzing trends quickly, using results that may be based on small but key samples that can accept or reject the null hypothesis. Analyzing the solution using these four questions can help you to objectify the risk you are taking, but they will not provide the total answer.

There are two more points to consider, the first less objective but just as important as the last. The gestalt, as psychologists refer to it, means looking at the total picture. In relation to risk, looking at the big picture means that you, as a visionary leader, need to learn to use your intuition. You need to develop a gut feeling based on the data that you have available. Data is always the key, and we will be devoting an entire chapter to discussing the collecting, modeling, and monitoring of data. For purposes of this discussion, however, you need to remember that data includes both objective and subjective elements. These elements include feelings, trend analysis from your customers, literature analysis, and review of key mentors' information. As we say, this is where the rubber meets the road; this is where you decide to make things happen or back off. This is the point of visionary leadership. Remember that risk is one of the most feared tools in a leader's toolkit, and I believe this is due to the fact that most of us don't trust ourselves or our gut reactions. If you have done your homework, completed your research, and looked at trends in relation to value to your customers, then you need to begin understanding and building confidence in yourself and in your ability to make sound decisions on the fly. This will take time, because risk self-confidence doesn't come overnight, but you need to develop this internal system for risk measurement. There is no easy way to develop this except through practice. Experience will help you to develop this level of confidence. It is your best teacher, and it will help you to develop your internal risk measurement system.

Finally, as a change agent you will need to develop a set of guiding principles when taking risks, and visionary ideas must *always* stand their test before you proceed. If a vision does not stand the test of your principles, strategies, and visions, then how can you expect others to believe in you as a visionary leader? If you have not thought about your absolutes, your "non-compromisable" principles, then now is the time to do so. You will never be a visionary leader if you don't stand for something. These statements or principles are what you will be known for and remembered by, and they will transcend the test of time. If you don't know them and constantly reiterate them, how can you expect others to know them? When you advance a new idea, it must first be tested against those principles as you evaluate the risk level and your tolerance for that risk.

Let me review and step you through the guiding principles that worked for me. You can use them in total, or with some modification thereof, or not at all. Whichever ones you choose, they must be yours, and you must believe in them or they will never work. You will notice that the principles I use are simple and straightforward.

My first principle is one that you have already heard. That is, I will take enough risk to be first to the market. This is critical if, as a leader, you are going to define the future for your customers and help them to solve what is wrong with their world. If the idea is already out there, it probably is no longer visionary unless you are using a new adaptation of that idea. Now, you can be first to market with an idea, but caution is necessary. Ideas that have no substance or plan behind them are, at best, just ideas. This is important, because our society needs leaders who will change our environment; and if you are not out in front, then I contend that we are simply rehashing what already exists rather than being creative. You will notice that I listed this as my first principle because that is the importance and value I attach to it. Many of the examples that I outline in this book reflect that principle.

Secondly, I will take risk only when the idea has substance from the data, subjective and objective, that I have collected, analyzed, and synthesized into a plan. That does not mean that you have to think things to death or, even worse, become paralyzed by the process; but you have to be comfortable with the idea and must have analyzed the trends that are out there, because you and you alone will have to defend them. Plan your thinking on paper so that you are consistent in how, what, and when you do things.

This is also the point where mentors, experts, the internet, and especially the data you have collected, no matter how minimal, will have an impact. When implementing projects considered risky, I would always rely on experts in the field to add credibility to my risk. When working on nanotechnology, I brought experts from the field to our city to tell the story. They gave credibility to the risk when the "trigger was pulled."

My third principle is consistency of purpose. I keep emphasizing trends because they are so very important. Logical consistency of response will allow you to lead with vision and do it with confidence. Does the new idea fit into your plan, your gestalt, your direction, and your modeling? Does it feel good in your gut and fit with what others know you to be? Does it follow the pattern that you utilize to accomplish things? It might be risky, but does it fit the big picture of who you are and what you stand for?

I remember making organizational changes shortly after I became president because changes had to be made for the survival of the college. I determined what changes would add value to the organization, talked with my mentor group of CEO's, analyzed the data, made the decision, and proceeded. Obviously, when you make changes in an organization that has been relatively stable for years, you create concern– and I did! The easiest thing to do in the face of criticism is to modify or change directions, but that is the worst thing you can do. If you have done your homework, stick with it, and it will work out. Now that doesn't mean that you don't make operational changes, because you may need to. Any plan will need tweaking, and that needs to be done. As my father used to say, "Remember, you can't eat principles," meaning that you should never get so tied to your idea that you will not make the operational changes that are necessary. Your basic framework, however, should stay consistent.

I am also a believer that I shouldn't take risks that I am not willing to see to completion, and that is my fourth guiding principle. I see many leaders who take a new position, make risky changes, and then move on before the changes take root. I have seen many organizations in a state of turmoil because they spent a great deal of time looking for a new leader who came on board, made risky or significant changes, and then moved to a different job before the changes were totally internalized. The organization then started all over, and the cycle continued. That type of behavior can delay the forward progress of an organization for many years. This type of behavior may look good on your resume, but in my mind it doesn't smack of good leadership; however, that is one you have to decide on because it can also slow up your career. If you truly believe in adding value to an organization and its customers, you as a visionary leader will seriously ponder this principle.

My principles are simple and straight forward, and they have been tweaked over years of experience. You have to develop your own guiding principles because you cannot just adopt mine or anyone else's because they are convenient. You have to believe in them and, most importantly, you need to live them. Because you will be following a plan of attack, the principles you adopt will take some of the risk out of risk-taking; but you must come to grips with the idea that visionary leaders are on the cutting edge and are open to criticism, potential failure, and in some cases lack of support. The following chapters will outline more of the tools that will help you to become comfortable with risks. They will remove the mystique and add objectivity to the world in which you will be living.

Step Three –
The Magic within your Crystal Ball–Data

If you don't measure it, you can't change it.

You are probably asking yourself, so what if I know what people need? How does that give me the vision to determine the value-added solution? The quick answer is that it does not because you have yet to do your research. You will need to collect and analyze your data; that becomes the next step in visionary leadership. I have discussed the use of data as an important tool for the visionary leader; this chapter is designed to help you to understand and utilize this tool in new and different ways. In order to determine the ultimate solutions, you will need to become competent in data synthesis that utilizes forecasting models.

While we know data is the key to success as a visionary leader, many leaders talk a good game but few truly know how to manage data for their benefit. Arguments or debates have been won because one party was able to give irrefutable data to support a position. In the same vein, many debates have been lost because the leader was not able to support the argument and was basing the debate purely on assumptions.

Data analysis is a topic that should be at the top of the agenda for all leaders and organizations, because the individuals that know how to use and analyze data are the ones that will succeed. As a leader of an organization you should certainly know how to access and analyze data, but you should also insist that all individuals in leadership roles in your organization know how to access and analyze data.

A wise trustee once told me, "If you can't measure it, you can't change it." He was right. Let me share some examples with you. As I implemented the business-based financial model at the college, the leadership staff was trained in marketing, growth trends, customer orientation, strategic planning, budgeting, and all of the familiar aspects of running a business or an organization. The strategic-planning process was streamlined and tied directly to budgeting so that we would end up with a goal for the organization in terms of "production" and a budget to support that production. Those were all correct steps, except for the fact that when I implemented them we then waited to see the results at the end of each semester and at the end of the year! Many were happy with this approach. Because there was no perceived pressure, they felt the result was out of their control. To say the least, this behavior was extremely frustrating to me as a leader; but as I learned in the quality movement of the seventies, the fault rested with me.

Remember the relationship between measurement and change? "If you don't measure it, you can't change it." Well, that is exactly what needed to happen but had not. My leaders did not have the tools or the challenge or the visionary leadership to do their job! I had not led with vision—a very sobering realization, to say the least. I waited patiently to see the results rather than working the plan to make the results we needed. Sound familiar? If at the end of the year the appropriate results had not been achieved, I would regroup and try again the next year. I know that this same thing occurs in many organizations and businesses around the world. When things don't change, it is blamed on many things, including complacency of staff. There is a common statement that you hear among the higher education community. It goes something like this: "When the economy is down, enrollments are up, and vice versa," This is easy justification for lack of vision and lack of a business plan! I am also convinced that is not just limited to the public sector. Many private-sector businesses are confronted with this same lack of vision, and leaders are ready to blame others for their lack of leadership. In many ways we have not learned the lessons taught by the quality gurus like Edwards

Deming, Phillip Crosby, and others. These individuals emphasized that most problems are a result of poor management and that the finger of blame usually points right back at us!

Now, realistically speaking, there are issues that complicate the situation, and those issues usually involve the availability of and access to data. We are in the information age, but as many of us know, the systems that have emerged are not always as user friendly as we expect them to be. Many of our systems are home grown, while others are very basic with few frills. As a result, we rely on information technology experts on staff for access to needed data, and those departments quickly become over-taxed. The resulting response from those departments has been to request more staff or ask leadership to prioritize their needs! Sound familiar? The complaint of leadership quickly becomes one of not being able to get the data or reports as promptly as they are needed, and thus business continues as usual in spite of problems that are hidden by the inability of systems or people to keep up.

Today that is no longer the case, or at least it shouldn't be! Let me take you back to my own situation. Was it complacency of the leadership staff? No, I had to accept the reality that it was not! Remember the "value" component that was discussed earlier? Many times it is hard to swallow, but value is determined by our customers, and that was true in this case. I had not listened and had not determined what was important for them to do their job. Therefore, I was not able to lead with vision. My staff was not saying that they needed more data; rather, they were not able to get to the point that I wanted them to with the tools available to them. They gave me a pocket veto because they were not able to analyze data as rapidly as I needed them to. What is a pocket veto, you ask? It is what I refer to as passive acceptance given to an idea; the staff nods approvingly but does not move forward. As a leader I knew that I needed data on production, on unit costs, and on trends on a daily basis, and I needed to be capable of breaking the data down by division of the college if I was going to be able to create the accountability necessary. If I couldn't get what I needed, how could I expect my staff to follow?

Today, you have tools that help significantly with this step. Business-intelligence tools and more elaborate systems like data warehousing can make the job of analyzing and predicting very easy *and*, above all, more user friendly. There should be no excuse for not using data to analyze and predict trends. You as a visionary should be capable of measuring and changing things! Data can be stored in formats that allow the comparisons necessary over time for leaders both to see trends and to analyze the impact of changes they have made. Probably the most significant advancement in these new tools and systems is that they allow end-user leadership staff to analyze data and create reports on their own, giving them greater freedom from information technology departments.

These systems can be pricey, but the cost of not implementing these tools can be even greater, resulting in staggering losses in productivity for an organization. Just implementing the tools and systems, however, will do no good if the leadership staff is not trained to use them consistently. Data analysis is so critical to visionary leadership in an organization that it must become an ongoing part of the training program for you and for every member of your leadership team. Similarly, you and your staff must use the tools in presentations. And remember, if you as their leader don't know the tools extremely well, the entire program is lost. You must walk the talk! Again, using my organization as an example, leadership training programs were held quarterly, and each of those sessions had a segment devoted to data utilization and analysis. Similarly, presentations at cabinet, staff, and trustee meetings were required to incorporate the use of the data-analysis tools. Leaders had to be able to use those tools as easily as they used pen or pencil.

It worked! We measured things daily and weekly, and we changed things. We grew when the economy was poor, and we grew when the economy was good. In fact, we became the fastest-growing college in our state and one of the top fifteen fastest growing colleges of our size in the nation. We tracked trends and we tracked results. We tracked costs and we tracked efficiencies. Many mid-level leaders became comfortable doing

Step Three – The Magic within your Crystal Ball–Data

things that are reserved for top management in many organizations. Nevertheless, I also had to realize that some leaders could not make the transition. These individuals had to move on if the organization was to be successful in this new environment. Access to data, along with the right tools and the training to use them, gave organizational leaders the ability to determine the right solutions. Value to others, new ideas, and a glimpse or vision of the future came as result of this access to data. Fears and anxieties turned into pride and accomplishments.

It does not end there, however. Your journey into visionary leadership has just begun. Remember, part of this step is forecasting, and this is where real visionary leaders are born. You are expected to have access to the proverbial "crystal ball." During my career more people have asked me about models or processes for determining future programs, products, ideas, and needed resources than about anything else. We are all concerned about the future and about being prepared for it–and rightfully so. Since none of us has access to the "crystal ball," we can dispense right away with that idea of magic. Visionary leaders need to utilize the data that is available to them if they are going to be successful. But just accessing that data is not going to do anyone any good. You must take a hint from our previous chapters and find new ways of applying existing ideas. We know that today's data-warehousing systems give us access to data in ways that were never before possible.

When I started in this business, computers were bigger than my office, and we used punch cards to process registrations. In most community colleges, computers were utilized in very limited processes and for the most part were accessible only to business office and student services staff. Any collection of data required a lot of time, effort, and manual calculation. Today, however, that has all changed! Computers carried in our pockets allow us to work wonders and access things never before possible. The problem for today's leaders is different. Many have not mastered the world of electronics. Some fear it; others rely on experts to do the work for them. If you are to become a visionary leader, you have to become the master of your own destiny. You do not have to become an information technology professional, but you need to have a solid working knowledge and understanding of the electronic world. If you do not, you will be setting yourself up for many problems in today's environment ranging from fraud to incompetent vendors. Most of all, you will not be ready to compete and reach your maximum potential. My word to you is not to fear the electronic era but rather to embrace it. If you want to become a visionary leader, you will have to walk the talk and teach others if you expect them to be a part of your team. If you want data to support your risk taking, you have to be willing to analyze, synthesize, and, most importantly, forecast. These are the tools of the trade, and you must know how to access and use them on a daily basis.

    I struggled with data throughout my career, not because I was afraid of computers but because I was not able to get what I felt I needed to do the job right. I have already explained the frustrations of dealing with IT departments that were over burdened and dreadfully slow in turnaround time. I would usually seek out individuals who had the same passion I did and work with them to "home grow" programs. Early in my career I was involved in learning styles and cognitive style mapping. I wanted to utilize individualized student data on a college-wide basis to help faculty adapt materials to the learning styles of their students. If you know learning styles, then you realize that associated mapping inventories are complex and require a great deal of interpretation. That complexity translates into a great deal of extra staff time and causes the demise of many worthwhile projects. That did not deter me, however, and I was able to latch on to a programmer who enjoyed this type of work. Together the two of us developed algorithms in a computer program that could generate a description of a student's learning style from the inventory input of that student. The resulting program worked well, allowing us to match alternative modes of instruction with individual learning styles and do it for all students without adding staff! In today's environment such things can be done more easily due to significant advancements in technology and software. As a visionary leader, you must always be looking for new ways to utilize that technology to create a better organization. I cannot

Step Three – The Magic within your Crystal Ball–Data

emphasize the importance of knowing and utilizing data and mastering technology. If you are not comfortable in this arena, then gaining such mastery is your first step.

In today's environment there are many consulting firms available to assist you, and I have utilized them successfully to keep my organization on the cutting edge. You can rely on consultants; but consultants must be considered as employees, and you will need to give them directions just as if they were members of your own staff. If you are not comfortable in this role, you could be led down pathways that can cost your organization millions! I recall a major university system that had been using outside consultants to develop a payroll system. They moved through several firms and raised the ire of the legislature and citizens as well because they did not take control of the situation. You do not want this type of problem. As a visionary leader, you must be master of your own destiny by understanding what you are working with, and it is not that difficult! I am not going to deal with the technology competence issue in this book, for in my estimation that is a prerequisite for visionary leadership. If you are not there now, you must get there as soon as possible.

As I continue to explore the use of data in visionary leadership, I am basing my discussion on the concept of measurement and change. Obviously, your first step is to determine what data you need. Remember, there is a lot of data available, but you need to be capable of narrowing the scope of what you are looking for or it will seem like an insurmountable task. Always keep in mind the concept that "garbage in" results in "garbage out," so don't take this seemingly benign step lightly. Determine what you need to do your job, and do it well. To accomplish this objective, you have to ask the question, "In an ideal world, what would I want to have at my fingertips every morning when I come to my desk?" In the language of today's technology, that information is referred to as your "dashboard." Your car's dashboard gives you the information to make immediate and long-term decisions at a glance. Your leadership dashboard should do the same. If your oil pressure is too low, a light comes on to signify the need to do something immediately. You will want those key checkpoints for your organization as well. What are some checkpoints? I will tell you what I experienced, but you will need to do some introspection to determine what you need in order to do your job effectively as the leader of your organization.

I was frustrated by my inability to get the organization moving in a positive direction because I was not able take accountability down to the level of individual courses. If I could not readily measure the effect of actions taken, then I could not determine if budget was being well spent. It was difficult to make changes if I couldn't explain the resulting impact. I wanted to know the enrollments of the college division by division, and I wanted to be capable of relating those figures to expenditures on a real-time basis just as a business is able to determine costs by product line on a real-time basis. Now I am here to tell you that most educational organizations do not operate that way. They deal with this type of data on a quarterly, semester, or yearly basis, and therein lies the problem. I knew that if I operated that way, I was always going to be dealing with lagging indicators and that I would not be able to make decision-based running changes.

I struggled to find answers to what seemed to be a simple question. Fortunately, with the help of a consulting firm, I came across a program that was able to move us in that direction. Business-intelligence software enables users to extract corporate data, analyze it, and then assemble reports. By working with outside help, the college was able to develop a dashboard containing critical data based on the sets of data that we were collecting. It allowed us to refine these sets of data, and it also gave us the option of looking at this data historically ("drilling down," as we say in the vernacular) to determine the effect of certain decisions. The software also allowed us to cross reference the data with other sets of data. For example, I could check enrollments against expenditures on a real-time basis. The downside was the consistency of the data over time. For example, if at some point in the past I had changed our operations, the inputted data was only available back to the time of the change. This limitation was not a major drawback, but it is one to keep in mind if you use these types of analytical software.

The other problem with the basic types of analytical software is that you are limited to categories of data that you determine. Setting up these categories does take time, but it is certainly worth the investment. Today, data warehousing takes this to new levels. A data warehouse is a repository of an organization's electronically stored data. Data warehouses are designed to facilitate reporting and analysis. They allow the end user to extract, transform, and load data, and to manage the data dictionary. Data warehousing includes business-intelligence tools; tools to extract, transform and load data into the repository; and tools to manage and retrieve data. All of this gives you both the control you need over the data of the organization and the ability to lead and make decisions on a real-time basis. You now can have the ability to determine the leading indicators, and you can see the effect of implementation on your organization.

When I implemented the dashboard and business-intelligence software, I was able to study the effects of change on the college and to analyze any division of the college. For example, I was able to determine and compare progress in the health division with similar progress in the trades division. I could determine what was working in one area and then transport that action to other divisions. This implementation did not come easily; it generated a great deal of anxiety among my leadership staff. Prior to implementation, progress and performance had been isolated from inspection because of a lack of data or lack of access to data. As real-time performance became available and could be viewed by everyone, not everyone was comfortable. Many viewed it as a performance evaluation and as threatening to their job security.

I established a rather large executive cabinet at the college because I believe that communication is a key to making things happen. While sheer numbers do not ensure positive results, sharing plans with more individuals helps as you go through rapid and expansive change as we did at the college. I feel it is important to have all of the people who affect the ultimate decision involved in discussing that decision. This involvement slowed us down at times, but in the final analysis it gave us the output we needed, and people could not say they didn't know what was happening. This was especially true when we implemented the business-intelligence software and introduced a new way of looking at the college.

As a visionary leader, you need to ensure that your staff knows how to use the data systems, because a key component of this approach is to have leadership and other staff members generate their own reports and data instead of relying on information technology experts to develop reports for them. This will require a great deal of attention on your part, at least during the implementation and training phases. First of all, you must become totally familiar with the software and know how to use it. You cannot pass this responsibility off to a vice president or anyone else, because if you do not walk the talk, you can forget about your staff doing it. They will view it as not being important to you and give you a pocket veto on the entire project. That being said, you will never become a visionary leader if you don't first take the lead.

Now, I am not ignorant when it comes to technology, but I am by no means a professional in that area. Needless to say, I spent a great deal of time studying the area and working with the experts so that I could use the software fluently. Then and then only could I feel comfortable requiring the same of my staff. I began by holding monthly training sessions as a part of our regular weekly leadership team meetings. We would cover a topic and then review that topic by having people utilize the new skill the next week. For example, I would ask these same staff members to use the skill when presenting at a cabinet meeting or even a board meeting. I want to digress for a moment to discuss something that I feel is critical to the entire process of becoming a visionary leader. Perhaps you noticed that I referred to my team as a leadership team and not as a management team. It is critical, I believe, for you to utilize terminology and actions that give people a "feel" for what they are trying to achieve. It may be a small part of the bigger picture, but words and actions are critical to success.

Step Three – The Magic within your Crystal Ball–Data

I eventually moved to the step of requiring that any reporting be done using the business-intelligence software. For example, we would report on organizational progress at our board meetings using the dashboard as a basis. This meant that I had to educate our trustees on how to use the software as well. As staff became familiar with the tools, we moved to the next step. During our leadership meetings we began to look at each of the divisions on a weekly basis. This raised anxiety levels, because for the first time leadership staff had to "bare their souls" in front of peers and senior leaders. The data was now available in real time and, of course, these division leaders were asked to explain how they got to that point. At first there were a lot of excuses that came forward; but as time went on, leadership staff began to really look into the data and became more comfortable with explanations.

Eventually, sharing of ideas came about, and only then did the anxiety begin to subside. This did not happen in days but rather in months, and it required the trust and understanding that I was not going to penalize staff for their standing but use it to help them do better. That is perhaps the most important concept for you to internalize. You can not penalize people for utilizing data and data systems; rather, you must help them to learn and understand what is happening as viewed through the data. Continuous training is a key to make these systems viable, and it cannot end with just one training session or when leadership staff has a cursory knowledge of the system.

After a year, staff began to really feel comfortable with the dashboard and with this way of looking at their world through new data. Then and only then did I begin to explore ways of using the new data for planning purposes and goal setting. Previously, the college had set production goals, but never had we set goals at the division level, nor had we budgeted according to division goals. Now I began able to use linear regression analysis to model and project outcomes on a division basis, using the information to determine whether the projected goals were realistic, too ambitious, or not ambitious enough.

It became extremely interesting to listen to the reasoning and projections that a group of people can come up with once they have access to historical data and are able to project models based on those trends. This is where creativity begins to happen and true visionary leadership begins to occur. Keep in mind that you, as a visionary leader, must lead this process. This process is your key to success, and you will quickly learn how to add value for your customers through this process. Bring back those key elements of watching, listening, and processing what you see, and most of all watch for the moments of creativity that need to be captured. Those new creative ideas that come forward will inspire everyone and help you to determine where you need to go, because now you are getting to where the real action is.

As time went on, staff became more comfortable with creating new dashboard elements because they knew it would help them to do a better job. There is always something missing in this process, because the real world is not linear and does not follow a linear projection. The real world, as we all know, is local, and it reacts to circumstances that are real-time based. Our leadership staff was now looking for more. Having had a taste of business intelligence and its power, they were ready for the next step. The next step was forecasting the future! They wanted to project the future not on a linear projection but on a real-world basis. We all know that the proverbial crystal ball does not exist, but our customers assume that we have access to one, or at least that our backgrounds allow us to see the future better than they can. I really struggled with this. Yes, we had a great system, we had access to a lot of data, and we had done a lot of training, but the planning process still seemed like too much of a guessing game for me.

My concerns took me towards modeling; and while a lot has been done with modeling, nothing seemed to work with our system. I am sure that many of you have had the same feelings. Great systems might be available, but they all seem very vague when it gets right down to your organization or business. I also felt that the planning process needed to be real, not just an exercise that ended up with a little-utilized document.

This left me with one alternative: to design a system that would work as a crystal ball.

I wanted a system that would bring in actual data, such as regional job openings that related to the various divisions of the college; that projected the matriculation of regional high school graduates and retention rates by college division; and that projected revenue from all sources and actual costs per full-time student. The overall system should be able to model the five future years based on the entered data and also allow for the insertion of "what if" data elements at selected points. These variable data elements would allow the model to recalculate the outcome in terms of needed budget and corresponding shortfalls or overages. The intent was to use this system as a tool, a means of adding realism to the process of planning and budgeting, and to end up with a useable product.

The model that resulted was built up from the division level. This strategy allowed divisions to do their own modeling based on the same data and then to aggregate it to the college level for budgeting and planning. As a result, each division of the college began to look at the career opportunities in the region and to determine which of those opportunities they needed to prepare students for in the ensuing years. The system utilized department of workforce regional data, extrapolating from that data the corresponding career opportunities that related to our educational opportunities. This has an interesting side note in that this caused divisions to look at career opportunities in the region and to relate those opportunities to programs in existence at the college. In terms of a system for determining needed career programs, it eventually resulted in the development of new programs based on this data. Staff were now looking outside of the box. For the first time they could relate the external world to their own division or department and experience those "aha!" moments. The downside is that the data from workforce development lags behind the current time period, sometimes by as much as two years. This necessitates the input of more current information at the division level from other resources, both regional and national.

Obviously, any revisions to the base data must be closely monitored to avoid compromising the data.

Once the data elements are entered, the algorithms of the model take over to aggregate and process the data. These algorithms were developed locally to ensure realistic modeling, and we spent a great deal of time creating them and tweaking them to meet our needs. Future years are predicted by entering anticipated changes to the data elements; of course, the further out the model is carried, the less accurate the data becomes; thus it is necessary to update the information at least annually, or more frequently if a source warrants it.

Once modeling is implemented, your planning sessions as a visionary leader become real. The sessions are no longer wishing or dreaming sessions. Wish lists can be put into real scenarios, resulting in numbers of students needed and resources to be allocated. The model then carries this forward to future years so that the full impact can be seen in real time. Then, if the numbers don't work out, you can determine what will work utilizing the "what if" features available to you.

Modeling is perhaps the greatest tool you can utilize. It gives everyone a look at the effects of change right on the spot; it takes away the ability of people to advance ideas without studying the implications; and it gives you the ability to find new ways of making critical decisions by analyzing new revenue streams through the reallocation of resources. Suddenly, the future is not so vague and intangible. You now can tie historical data and projections to the effect of future ideas through modeling.

There are, however, shortcomings to modeling. Remember the "garbage in, garbage out" symptom that was discussed earlier? That is especially true for modeling. As a visionary leader, you must make certain that the algorithms of the model are as accurate as possible. Achieving this kind of accuracy requires more than a one-time review; rather, it is the result of an ongoing process. Retention rates, enrollment-to-graduate ratios, attraction rates, and revenue percentages must constantly be updated. Furthermore, it is essential that staff constantly review any externally inputted data for currency and accuracy. Others may be critical of your model, and that is good. Criticism allows you to review your values and motives through introspection, and that is a necessary part of visionary leadership. Remember, it is better to have people question the algorithms you are using than to criticize you for a lack of vision!

The neat thing about modeling is that it becomes your crystal ball. If you use it properly, it will provide you a composite picture of the future that you and your leadership staff develop together. Modeling is great because it covers multiple years! As you play out a "what if" scenario in one year, the budget and enrollment implications are carried forward so that you can see the effect in future years. Too many times leaders look only at the current budget year. Their behavior can be compared to the experience of learning to drive a car. At first you looked only at the road in front of the car, but eventually you learned to look further down the road. Modeling allows you as a visionary leader to look further down the road. Looking at future impacts can help you with risk taking as well, because now you can see the impact of that risk and determine if it fits into your risk-tolerance boundaries.

As I indicated in the beginning of this chapter, data is critical and should become your best friend; but as a visionary leader, you must remember two things. First of all, you must always validate data with your first-hand knowledge of the situation. Do not be afraid to override data if what you observing does not validate the numbers. Remember that as a visionary leader you are not paid to follow numbers alone. If that were the case, anyone could do your job. You are being paid to take the organization forward, to take necessary risks while keeping things solvent. Since that is your role, you must not only look at the data but also trust the skills you have developed. Second, you must be selective in the data that you surround yourself with. Too much data is just as bad as too little or no data. Many people can produce fact after fact but are not able to use that information. As a visionary leader, your role is to use data, not just produce it. You will also stifle the creativity of you leadership team if you confront them with too many data variables. It is your job as a visionary leader to determine the boundaries within which your team operates, and that includes data. Keep it simple and concrete! It is no different than the lengthy strategic plans that exist in many organizations but which are so broad that no one can get a grasp of them.

Modeling, business-intelligence software, and data warehousing are all great tools; but as with anything else, just installing them does not solve the problems. That is where leadership, *your* leadership, comes in. Your staff and your customers will look to you to anticipate the future and use the necessary data properly. That takes us full circle to the beginning, back to the statement that "if you can't measure it, you can't change it." You know now that you can measure things. The real challenge for you as visionary leader is changing things. These tools can help you to become more comfortable with risk by adding objectivity to your world. While it is not magic, data will in fact become your crystal ball if you learn to understand and use it well. Always remember that magic is only part of the picture. You need to be capable of putting everything together to become that visionary leader.

In the next step we will be dealing with a component that will become your gestalt as a visionary leader. That chapter deals with the development of your plan. It is where everything starts to come together.

Step Four –
Making Your Vision Real–Modeling the Plan

It's all about the bottom line.

When I started my position as president and CEO, I inherited a rather elaborate strategic-planning process. A planning committee was selected each year from the various ranks within the college and included a trustee. External data was collected and presented to the committee, along with plan additions proposed by staff members. After spending several months considering the proposals and the data, the committee made recommendations as to which of the items would be included in the plan. The plan was then presented to a small, hand-chosen community advisory committee for review, then to the internal staff and, finally, to the trustees for approval. From there the college went on to budgeting, using the strategic plan as a tool.

On the surface this looked like a process that had merit–that is, until I looked at the utilization and the input. The external input was minimal at best, and the resulting document was so large and so broad that staff could include just about anything in the budget and be confident that it was supported by the strategic plan. When I asked staff about the plan, they could not tell me what was in it, referring to it only as "that document." It was an annual process that everyone felt obligated to do, but one that carried very little, if any, credibility. I am here to tell you that this approach is not unusual in colleges or businesses. Everyone knows you need a strategic plan, but many do not value it as a working document.

I have emphasized that visionary leaders need a plan and that they need to follow that plan with consistency if they are going to be successful. Let's look at the makeup of a sound plan and process. Previously I have discussed data availability, analysis, and forecasting; and if you subscribe to that thinking, you should be not have to look beyond your desktop to get the data necessary to begin this total process. Most importantly, the process that I am going to set forth must be an ongoing process as opposed to one which occurs at a set time each year. If you are not asking your staff to plan on a year-round basis, how can you expect your organization to have the agility to rapidly respond to external influences? Those influences don't occur once a year; rather, in a vibrant organization they are constantly emerging. As a visionary leader, you must be ready to review the input and then respond, moving your organization into these new directions. First to market is key! I have chosen to call this process a business plan rather than a strategic plan for that emphasis if for no other reason. Let's begin to dissect the business plan with the idea in mind that a visionary leader will need to be comfortable with the process as opposed to simply adopting someone else's plan. Some key elements need to exist in any plan, and that is what we will cover in this step.

Perhaps the most important element in the business plan is CEO involvement. It galls me when I see planning processes where the CEO introduces the session and leaves, only to be seen when it is finally over. That really sets the stage for the importance of the process! As a visionary leader, you must understand that this is and must be YOUR process! You must believe in it and consider it to be the map for your organization. If you don't, it will surely be relegated to obscurity.

Secondly, in the last paragraph I used the words "when it is finally over." It must never be over! It must be an ongoing process, one that captures the creativity of your organization and stimulates it to take the necessary risks and respond rapidly to the needs of your customers.

Third, the process must be externally oriented, drawing together

Step Four – Making Your Vision Real–Modeling the Plan

the concerns and ideas of your constituency, the customers you are in business to serve. I see way too many planning processes that rely almost exclusively on internal input. Remember, if you are going to be a visionary leader, you must determine what is of value to the people who rely on your organization. This does not mean you ignore internal input, but you must give external input the highest level of importance.

Fourth, the process and the resulting documentation must be simple and understandable. The old elevator speech comes to mind. You and your staff should be able to describe where your organization is going in the time that it takes an elevator to move up or down one floor. If your plan is lengthy and complex, it will never get done because of a lack of understanding. Without that understanding, you can expect to receive pocket vetoes on a regular basis, and that is exactly what you do not want. So to be useable, the business plan must be brief and understandable.

Fifth, the plan must actually provide direction. It should not be words on paper but marching orders for you, the visionary leader, and for your staff. It must be real to you, to your staff, and especially to your customers. Everyone must believe in the direction enough to allocate resources to make it happen. Too many times I would hear people say, "That is a terrific idea." But when I would ask which resources they were willing to give up to make it happen, they would back off rapidly. No idea should make it into the plan unless the organization is willing to reallocate existing resources to make it happen. These items must be important enough so that the resources for them come "off the top" before the budgeting process begins.

Sixth, and certainly not of least importance, is the use of and involvement of data. Using the "I think" mentality, it is easy to come up with great ideas in the process; but unless they have a real basis in data, they should not be considered. Remember, unless you are able to measure the impact of the idea on the organization, you will never know if the money was well spent.

This is really where you begin to earn your money as a visionary leader. The normal tendency of leadership staff is to back off on reallocating resources, and thus we get into the proverbial status quo that many organizations face. So how do you prevent that from happening? You must lead, and that means you must set the parameters within which planning and budgeting occur. That is your job and yours alone. You need to set the expectations, determine the tools available, outline the process, and set the rules of engagement. Then and only then can you begin to plan.

Let's look at a real-life example of building a business plan. I will take you through the plan I used to transform the college that I have been discussing throughout this book.

The planning process I will be describing runs year round, but as with any process, it has a beginning and an end. The process revolved around a fiscal year (July through June), but it could be adaptable to a calendar year as well. With that in mind, the planning process should begin with public-input sessions. These sessions actually do double duty, providing a chance to tell the story of your organization to the public and then use that story as a means of gathering input for the plan. Since this process is year round, you should encourage input at anytime and provide electronic and other types of opportunities for commentary to occur including email and phone access. You should also expect leadership staff to gather input at available community opportunities, and you and your trustees should be accessible to the community for input.

Since the college covered a large region with multiple campuses, I always scheduled our input sessions at various locations convenient to the customers. It is critical that the visionary leader go to the customers' turf rather than the other way around. The input sessions were also held at times convenient for the customers, and I was always respectful of their time, limiting the sessions to no more than two hours. The size of the region necessitated seven sessions, and as president I attended and conducted each of them. Remember, it is important that external and internal customers understand that you consider this process important and valuable. We would advertise the sessions in the local media and send out invitations to key individuals in the area where the session was being

Step Four – Making Your Vision Real–Modeling the Plan

held. Each session began with a review of the vision and an explanation of the business model of the college. These elements were presented in a simple format so that people could understand and remember them. The local media in each of the areas were invited and given a preview of what was going to happen. They were also given personal time with me before or after the session to ensure that they could get the information they needed to do their job. You always want to accommodate the press, because anything they publish about your organization is free publicity for you. Make them your friends!

The sessions should include concrete data on the progress of the organization, utilizing the tools that you have implemented. I always presented the positive and negative outcomes, including what worked and what did not, and I fielded questions no matter how difficult the situation was. The remainder of the session should provide opportunities for structured input designed in a way to feed directly into the process. We also provided paper and electronic input so that attendees could submit information they thought of after the session. Finally, I allowed time for unstructured input so that the audience could ask or comment on anything about the organization that was concerning them at that time. It is important to collect address information from the participants so that you can continue to inform them about the process and outcomes on an ongoing basis. After all, these are people who are interested enough in your organization to voluntarily attend a meeting, and you will want to inform them about other aspects of your operation as well.

In addition to these external sessions, you will want to gather input from internal staff as well because they are another level of customer. These sessions should follow the same format so that you can more easily gather the data. I always reported raw data back to all participants for review before any processing began. This is important because it gives everyone involved a picture of what was of value to all customers, both internal and external.

In earlier chapters I discussed tracking trends. This input will give you the first chance to do that. At this point you should begin tracking ideas that came from multiple individuals. Even if this information is not extensive, you will then start to get an idea as to what was of value to your customers. If these sessions are structured correctly, you will be amazed at the ideas that come from them, and it is important to devise a system that allows you to easily track the data from year to year. You never know what you will discover!

The input should be aggregated in the respective categories in which it was collected. It should then be shared with the staff at the college, for this becomes the basis for the planning process. It is critical to always consider external input and give it more weight than internal input. I expected the divisions of the college to review the data with their staff, and, if appropriate, to develop a budget/planning response. If no response is warranted, reasons for the decision should be expected so that it can again be shared with the public. It is always important for you to cultivate the relationship with the public, a relationship that will deteriorate rapidly if the public feels you are not giving adequate consideration to their input. After all, they volunteered their time and they deserve a response. It also gives internal credibility to the process, for input cannot be dismissed without a valid reason.

As these responses were being prepared, we also asked the divisions of the college to begin updating the workforce data that pertained to their division. New data was available annually, and thus it was an appropriate time to review, update, and consider the workforce needs of the region. This data formed the basis for the modeling that was done at least annually as a part of the planning process. I also asked the divisions to review the workforce data that related to the programs they now offered to determine the number of job openings in the region. They were also asked to review job openings in reference to new program offerings that might work in the region. This review correlated with the information from the town hall meetings and gave each of the divisions the opportunity to develop their respective plans for budgeting purposes. You should construct your own workforce data based on regular availability and updates, on the needs of your region, on the acceptance

Step Four – Making Your Vision Real–Modeling the Plan

of the data in your region, and on the ease of utilization. Data which is not regional, current, and easy to use will soon be cast aside, and you will lose your forward motion.

One criticism of the process I used related to the use of regional data and to the fact that many students end up leaving the region. From a community college perspective, regional data is critical because of the service area of most community colleges. Secondly, I contend that the variance among regions is not that great, with the exception of specialty niches. In other words, most regions need business, healthcare, trades, information technology and service graduates, so the transportability for graduates and thus data is quite good.

The workforce data was translated into graduates needed from each division on an annual basis. This data was then aggregated into the forecasting model for utilization during the planning process. At this point I would begin the modeling process to see if we could in fact sustain the amount of increase that was being projected by the aggregated division data. We used "what if" scenarios to determine our penetration into the annual high school graduate market and to determine the growth that we wanted to achieve based on the number of our graduates that were needed in the region. The model then calculated the resources needed, and those calculations allowed us to determine what projects would be possible during the next budget cycle as well as their impact in future years. As you begin to use modeling, you will have to experiment with algorithms that work for you, for your organization, and for your region of the country. If you are not comfortable with constructing algorithms, find someone nearby who is and hire or use that person to help you. Computer programmers and programming students love this kind of work, so don't be afraid to recruit them. It may seem difficult, but the more you utilize algorithms and modeling, the more comfortable you will become. Remember, you do not have to construct the program, just the "if-then" statements that you want to utilize. You will also need to refine them over time if they are truly to become useable tools. An example of a simple algorithm might be,

"If we enroll x (number) of students, we will graduate x (number) two years later."

I insisted that every item brought forward by divisions be substantiated with backup information compiled into a one-page uniform format. This information included a description of the project along with the need for the project based on data and customer input. The document also included an activity timetable for implementation, expected measureable outcomes related to the college goals, the needed human resources, cost estimates (operational and capital), and the sources for any new expenditures. Divisions were required to look at all possible revenue sources, including internal reallocation within their divisions, grants, and new revenue generation before requesting new college-wide resources for the project.

It is much too easy to suggest ideas and expect others to come up with the necessary resources or to simply rely on new money. This is the point in many processes that leads organizations into difficulty. As a result, you will always want to ask each division or operational unit to develop a list of possible items for reallocation. Needless to say, this usually is not received with enthusiasm, and it may take time to get to the operational level you expect. I also aggregated capital expenditures on a separate list simply because our system utilized a different resource stream (bonding) for capital items. Because that process may not apply to all systems, you will need to deal with it in the appropriate manner.

I began the review of submissions early, and prior to the meeting each cabinet member was expected to review the submissions being considered each week and prepare to ask questions at the meeting. In order to save time, we did not review the entire project at the meeting. Our cabinet basically had five choices to make at the meeting, including leaving the item in the plan for new resources, leaving the item in the plan utilizing division generated resources, not implementing the item, moving it to a future year, or holding pending more information. An item could be put in the first category of requiring new resources only if everyone agreed that the item was absolutely necessary for the forward direction of the

Step Four – Making Your Vision Real–Modeling the Plan

college, and it would stay in the plan even if it meant reallocating existing resources elsewhere in the college. I am sure each of you can imagine the anxiety and concern that this caused, but it really helped to separate the "nice to have" from the "need to have" quite quickly.

One critical item, and the one that will take the longest to implement, is the expected measureable outcomes based on the organization's goals. The concept of measurement and change is difficult in any organization, especially if it is not expected and has not been utilized in the past. As I implemented the business-based model described in an earlier chapter, we developed five basic premises of operation based on customer input. These premises gave us general direction, albeit primarily on a financial and programmatic level. I will review them again at this point because they form the basis for measurement:

- Maintain operational reserve equal to 21% of Budget
- Control/reduce costs through process improvement
- Increase enrollments through growth programs
- Control budgets to maintain a buffer between available mill rate and budget mill rate
- Develop long-range capital and equipment plans

As you can see, these premises were formulated to transcend time and were very broad and general. The strategic goals were based on these premises and thus emphasized the direction of the college as outlined. The strategic goals were reviewed annually but, barring unusual circumstances, only changed on a three-to-five-year basis when the college did a major environmental scan. I will emphasize the fact that our goals did not change over a ten-year period even with continuous external and internal customer input. In my opinion, goals that cannot stand the test of time for at least five years are not truly strategic in nature.

Let's take a look at the long-range strategic goals that resulted from the business model:

- The college will meet the diverse and dynamic training needs of the region
- The college will meet changing student educational needs

- The college will enhance seamless transition for all students between educational systems
- The college will be fiscally and organizationally healthy

On the surface, these goals seem quite simple and straightforward, goals that any college worth its salt might seek to achieve. They, however, embody the essence of what you must consider as you develop your goals. First of all, they should be brief and concise so that anyone can remember them, internalize them, and utilize them. They should not be a fifty-page strategic plan that sits on the shelf! Secondly, you should be able to formulate measurements around them and follow those measurements over time to see if in fact you are making a difference. Thirdly, your yearly operational goals must support the strategic goals so that you can see the impact of annual changes on your direction.

Each of these goals had several measurements that were determined by college staff to be the marks of progress toward the goals. Those measurements became our dashboard and were reviewed weekly at cabinet meetings, monthly at board meetings, and at every possible professional development opportunity with all staff. Remember, communication and consistency are important characteristics of visionary leadership. It is much too easy to become lax in this arena and lose momentum entirely; and believe me, there is pressure in most organizations for this to occur. Countless times I had my own leadership staff attempt to diminish the need to review this data because of time constraints or the importance of other activities. I learned that if a goal is to rise to the level of strategic significance it must have everyone's attention and that I was the one who needed to continually emphasize that.

As yearly operational goals are developed, you will need to question how and to what extent they will impact the strategic goals. Although this process is somewhat subjective, expected outcomes must nevertheless be set at an appropriate level and then studied over time. If over time an operational goal is not affecting the organizational goal positively–or worse, is moving it in a negative direction–it must be considered for discontinuance. The time for this process is not a precise science, and subjectivity always enters the equation; but you are creating an atmosphere in which people are looking at leading and lagging indicators and dealing with accountability, and it must be done.

That leads to another important point associated with this type of planning and change. Failure is a part of this process and is not bad or negative. If, as a visionary leader, you do not create an atmosphere where others can take risks, you will never change the organization. If you truly utilize the tools available to you and work with staff to use data and to study impacts, you will be amazed at the level of competency that will develop in your organization and the corresponding pride that will result. If you use visionary leadership techniques, change can and will become a way of life.

As we worked our way through the operational change documents each year, they were always reviewed in relation to their impact on these strategic goals. Thus it became easier, though not simpler, to evaluate items brought forth to vie for budget resources. Obviously, some items could be easily judged; but the closer you got to a finished product the more difficult it became to discern one project from another. Once the change items were selected each year, we moved on to the budgeting process, following some of the same guidelines. If an item had been approved for new resources, it had to remain, even if it meant giving up something else that was previously in the plan.

A difficult part of the process is convincing staff to "clean house." By that I mean giving up existing processes, projects, or staff. The first thing that usually comes to mind is to use "zero-based budgeting," when you start each year with a clean slate and seek to justify everything. Obviously, as good as this sounds, it is very difficult or impossible in a large organization. You are faced with processes that must operate continuously from year to year, and thus zero-based budgeting is not a practical option. You can ask each unit to provide a percentage of its operation for reallocation; but if you are truly using visionary leadership, this does not make sense. You could be changing operations that in fact are moving your organization forward. This part of the process is not an exact science, and each of you will need to find out what works best for your organization; but it must be done or you will never move forward. The resistance to change in organizations is stronger than the desire to change. I used a process that was somewhat a combination of items. Each division was asked to review its operation and determine which items it could possibly reallocate. You would always hear the wailing and gnashing of teeth and people saying, "I can't possibly cut anything from my operation." As a visionary leader you cannot allow this, because this is symptomatic of the problems with many organizations today. If visionary change is to occur, we cannot continue to do things as they always have been done. As a visionary leader, you must lead the charge. I would not tolerate the pocket veto and insisted that divisions submit items for reallocation. Believe me, this was not popular. I would always use the leverage of taking an across-the-board cut from a unit if it did not come up with something. You will find that change is difficult for many of your leadership staff if they cannot look outside of the box. This is when you have to help them hear what customers are saying and then use the data and modeling options available to them. Remember, new directions will only occur if you are willing to take risks to add value to those who are your customers.

The final part of the process becomes one of converting your plan to budget. By the time you get to that point, it should become *pro forma*. With your plan well in hand and items prioritized, it should become just an exercise. Of course, you should be communicating your ideas with staff and trustees at various points throughout the process so that when the time comes for approval it is almost an accepted fact. And by all means, don't forget your customers! They need to know what happened to their input, and you will want to call on them in the future. It is your responsibility to keep them in the loop.

If you are truly going to be a responsive and visionary organization, this cannot be a once-a-year process. So how does that happen? This is the most difficult part of the process. When you plan your resources and budget, you in fact are making commitments to your staff and to the communities you serve. As a visionary leader you must prepare for the unexpected and be willing to make running changes. The Italian term *andiamo* comes to mind, which roughly translated means "on a dime." Today's organizations need to be able to turn on a dime if they are going to be competitive in the emerging markets of today's environment.

There are several ways in which rapid change can occur. I would always keep on reserve any projects offered by staff for reallocation but not utilized. These provide opportunities for future reallocation during the fiscal year. Obviously, budgeting in reserves also allows for that to occur, and at times that was also utilized. One of our premises, you will recall, was to maintain an amount equal to twenty-one percent of operations in reserve. I attempted to ensure we would be able to operate for at least six months if necessary and to be able to operate in an environment where resources arrived in uneven payments at various times throughout the fiscal year. The twenty-one percent was more than was necessary to meet that requirement, and therefore I had excess to use if necessary for running changes required to meet emerging needs.

A third way involved our foundation, a 501c (3) organization designed to support the college and its students. I created a fund within the foundation that was designed to provide seed money for emerging community projects in which the college might be expected to become involved. These funds were accessible only through the foundation board, thus avoiding any temptation to use them to meet budget shortfalls; and the projects had to meet very specific criteria, including repayment from college funds over time. This fund was set up to encourage risk, meet regional needs, and stimulate innovation. I personally raised funds from community business leaders who were supporters of the college and who understood the need to operate in an ever-changing environment.

So where did it all end up? Remember, I said I inherited a college that was experiencing declining enrollment, had insufficient operational reserves, was borrowing for operations, and had a high cost per student. In a period of three years we became one of the fastest-growing colleges of our size in the country, developed a twenty-five percent operational reserve, and moved to the lowest cost per student among the colleges in our state. And we were able to maintain that status!

More important than the statistics was the effect on college personnel. As leaders began to take risks and were willing to share within the college, they became justifiably proud of their work. They were asked to present at state and national forums, were recognized in the community and in the media, and became revitalized in their careers. Visionary leadership does pay off! I have often said that when parents, upon graduation, proudly profess in social situations that their son or daughter is going to a community or technical college, then we will have achieved our goal. Our college's status changed, and the community was proud to say that we helped to make our region a better place to live, work, and learn.

When your communities start to believe in you as a "value-adder," you will begin to know that visionary leadership does work, and then your real work begins. You, too, will have become a visionary, and those same communities will come to expect more from you in the future. You will always need to keep in mind that the visionary leader you are becoming is not a result of any innate or inborn ability. Rather, it is a result of following a consistent process based on careful planning and on taking calculated, data-based risks to add value to the customers that you are serving.

Step Five – Developing an Agile Leadership Team

*Feed them a fish and they eat for a day;
teach them how to fish and they eat for a lifetime.*

The opening quote, though well known, is especially true in visionary leadership. If you are going to be a visionary leader, you need a team of people working with you who understand your thinking and have similar convictions. Like the carpenter's house, higher education is many times woefully inadequate in preparing its own. We expect people to be well educated and ready to work in institutions like ours and therefore able to "hit the ground running." Wrong! Most institutions of higher education use an in-service model where faculty and leadership get together at the beginning of each academic semester, with little if any continuity from year to year. There might even be a leadership and support staff in-service program, but these programs usually cover emerging topics as opposed to ongoing leadership skill development. If you are to become a visionary leader, and if your organization is going to emerge as a leader, that trend must change. Just because it always has been done that way is no reason for it to continue. You must begin to practice what you preach! If ongoing education and training are critical for the people and industries that your organization serves, then they must become a staple for your staff and especially for your leaders.

Visionary leaders need to utilize quality processes in education, just as leaders do in manufacturing, healthcare, and other business sectors. I utilized this framework whenever possible at the college, and as you read this book you will see evidence of that process in every step that has been covered. Now there are many different processes that can be utilized, and as a visionary leader you need to be familiar with them in order to develop your own direction. Whether you utilize the Deming, Crosby, or some other approach, it is consistency that is critical in applying the principles. I personally believe that an eclectic approach is the best, because it allows you to choose the best from all of the processes and apply them to your organization.

Because the quality principles are so important to visionary leadership, we mandated a short twenty-hour training session for each and every employee, including support staff, custodial-maintenance staff, faculty, leadership, and trustees. These sessions covered the basic principles selected for utilization at our college by an internal task force that developed the operational quality process for our college. These were not just presentations; they utilized a prepared curriculum that included competencies and outcomes. Time was allocated during the workday, and the credits were useable for recertification or salary schedule advancement.

I do not believe that an organization should become fanatical about the process. I have seen very structured processes destroy all enthusiasm for the application. I do feel that simple awareness of the concepts breeds success and that, when this approach is used, staff will begin to use the processes in their departments on their own. We also provided voluntary advanced sessions that included the necessary training for staff interested in becoming facilitators. Over time, the processes permeated everything we did in the organization.

As a visionary leader, you will need to lead the charge and practice what you preach. At every opportunity—at in-service sessions, board meetings, or cabinet meetings—you should be prepared to utilize the principles that you adopt. They should become the very foundation of how you conduct business. Obviously, you have to be prepared for criticism. I remember situations in which a decision was made that went against a particular group of staff. Often the response was, "You talk quality but you aren't practicing it in this situation." You will be confronted with this type of comment, and you should not be rattled by it. If consistency of action and purpose is your mantra, in the long run you will prevail.

This brings up a key point in terms of leadership and the quality processes, and that point concerns the empowerment of staff. Obviously, the quality processes involve staff in decision making; however, it is still your role as the leader of the organization to set the direction and boundaries. Within those boundaries, staff becomes involved in determining how those directions will be met. As visionary leader, you must take the responsibility for outlining the direction; if you don't, your organization will flounder. You cannot abdicate your responsibility to set the stage for the organization. As I mentioned in an earlier chapter, if you fail to set the direction, empowerment will end when the tough decisions need to be made.

The quality processes must be the basis for educating your staff and an ongoing part of that education, but that is only the beginning for you as a visionary leader. You also need to review your business plan and use those projections to trigger the type of education and ongoing training that your staff will need. Of course, it will differ if your staff has been with you over time and is already familiar with the operation; but most organizations have enough annual turnover to warrant an ongoing familiarization program, and a review certainly will not hurt the senior staff. For purposes of this chapter, I am going to concentrate on leadership staff education, realizing full well that all staff needs to be familiar with the concepts. I believe that leadership staff needs to educate the staff that works for them, for that gives them the opportunity to use what they have learned. As you know, teaching a concept is the best way to learn it yourself. The training program I utilized was continuous, and the leadership staff was expected to participate, including the president!

I will discuss the program and get into content later. The leadership education program I implemented began each year with a weeklong event in the summer. It was usually held off campus to avoid distractions from the office, and the atmosphere was informal. During that week an education theme for the entire year was presented, along with a calendar of events complete with dates and times so everyone had ample time to get them scheduled. That calendar included a scheduled mixture of half-day and full-day sessions each month for the fiscal year. You may feel that that sounds like a lot, but remember, you either pay now or pay later! If you don't provide that education time for your staff, you will suffer lost time and lost productivity later on. I tried as much as possible to tie the sessions to dates when regularly scheduled meetings such as cabinet meetings were held.

I made certain that a manual was always prepared and distributed at the first session. This manual was to be utilized the entire year and was complete with schedules, bios of speakers, copies of presentation materials, and worksheets for each session. There is no substitute for a well-planned set of events. In no case should you ever throw an event together at the last minute. It would be better to not do it at all! I believe that staff education sessions should include competencies to be learned, including the performance standards expected. Remember, the same rules that we use for our students should apply to us. If your sessions don't come with expectations, they are probably not worth doing, so planning and preparation is a key. The same rules apply to any external speakers you are bringing in to consult with your organization. Too many times organizations bring in speakers and consultants who simply speak and leave. If you do not make a direct connection to learning, those sessions are a waste of your time and the time of your staff.

The initial weeklong sessions were designed to set the stage for the future of the organization, and I always tried to ensure that they were packed with valuable new information. If your staff feels that the sessions are a waste of time, you will have lost the impact and direction. This is your opportunity as a visionary leader to spend time with your staff discussing your leadership style and expectations. You really need to prepare in detail for this session, because your presentation will set the

Step Five – Developing an Agile Leadership Team

stage for your entire plan of work. Your leadership staff deserves to know you and your style in great detail, so get used to baring your soul. It goes with the territory. Being a somewhat private person, I had a difficult time with this at first, but over time I became comfortable with allowing others to know more about me. Stories about my upbringing on a farm and my interests in automobiles and, of course, anecdotes about my kids and grandkids seemed to make me more human to them. In the long run, this openness about myself helped them to understand more completely where and why I was taking the organization. Your time spent here will save countless hours of corrections and misunderstandings later. You will need to use all of your communication skills to portray the person you really are, so be prepared to do a lot of planning and homework, even practicing in front of video camera if necessary. I definitely do not recommend that you read a script. Instead, practice being yourself, reviewing what you said and how you said it. This can be invaluable!

If you have a mentor whom you identify with, this is also a great time to invite that person in as a keynoter to add credibility to your direction and story. If used correctly, this type of keynote address can be a great "kick off" to the week. But make absolutely certain that the person you utilize is a charismatic speaker, or you may regret utilizing this approach.

I would start the week with very general content. As the week progressed, I would move toward more specificity, making certain that everyone left with the organization's direction in mind. I always used these sessions to unveil a change for the organization, whether it was a change in a process, in a program, or in staffing. Over time, this added a tone of anticipation to these events because everyone wanted to hear about the latest and the greatest. I also utilized this same tactic with annual all staff in-service sessions, and it provided the same effect. It points to the need for you to personalize these sessions. You may use a different tactic that is more "you," but the key is to make certain that the sessions emulate your style and direction and that in the end staff view them as time well spent.

If you expect the participants to be prepared for the sessions, the week's agenda and materials should be available to all participants at least two weeks in advance. There were times I would expect prior preparation so that we could make the most effective use of the time, including collecting or preparing materials specific to their department to utilize and share during the week.

I utilized a lot of external organizations to do work at the college, because I am of the philosophy that education was the business of the college. Some operational aspects of a college can be done better, and many times less expensively, by external organizations. This is commonly called outsourcing, and I believe it allowed the college to stay on the cutting edge in many areas. More importantly, it helped significantly with my speed-to-market principle, because the work that was being done by these companies was their primary focus, just as ours was on education. Working together, we each had our areas of expertise, and the combination allowed the college to move forward faster than if we tried to be experts in all areas. Similarly, it meant that I had access to staff and consultants in many areas of expertise who had the very latest knowledge and skills needed for an emerging project and who could be brought in for as long as they were needed. Creating a staff and doing the training needed would have slowed progress considerably and provided much less flexibility or agility. I commonly outsourced things like the information technology department, call center, food service operation, parts department, book store, and the online-learning transition team.

The reason I bring up outsourcing in this chapter is not to advocate for outsourcing. I bring it up to make the point that, as a visionary leader, you cannot outsource a process and expect it to run itself. If you have that expectation, outsourcing will stand a good chance of failing. If it does not meet your expectations, most likely it is because you have not provided leadership. I treated external employees and companies as if they were part of my staff, and thus I expected all vendors and their employees to participate in our staff development programs as well as in on-campus meetings. I went so far as to include in my cabinet the heads of on-campus departments that were outsourced. Outsourced departments were given the same treatment, rights, and responsibilities as other departments. Therefore, as a part of their contract, the heads of outsourced units were expected to participate in these weeklong sessions as well. It had a side benefit in that it brought these individuals into the campus family, and that was critical to the success of these operations. If you utilize this approach, you may run into the concerns that internal staff members have about this involvement; but as a visionary leader you will need to stand tall for your decisions. I have found that most of the initial concerns about including these "external" individuals dissipate when others see the benefits they bring to the table and especially to their departments.

The most important outcome of these weeklong sessions was image development. I wanted and achieved the image that the college was a place to go if you really wanted to succeed in the world. I wanted it to be recognized as a place that students chose for exciting careers that might even be a capstone for baccalaureate degrees. Image change is difficult, because your leadership staff, and eventually all staff, must be convinced that it is fact. It is a product of having the right services, the right buildings and equipment, the right mix of programs, and the right faculty and staff to put it all together. That requires visionary leadership, and it begins with educating your leadership staff.

These sessions became marketing sessions to the staff as much as training sessions for them. As a visionary leader, you have to use your public relations skills at every opportunity to make this a reality. Once internal staff believe in you and the direction, the rest is easy. The kick-off for the week always included marketing what the organization was to become—my vision, if you will—and the entire first day was usually spent on this. It included my presentation on where the organization was heading, along with pertinent changes that could be expected. This was interspersed with well-chosen keynote speakers who could help to set the stage because they were intimately familiar with things that were happening on the global scene. Expanding horizons is especially critical if you plan to change the image of your organization. The last thing you want is for your staff to hear more of the same or to hear about only local happenings. You have an obligation to make the event a mind-expanding session, an experience that causes them to move beyond the shores of where they are to the realm of what might be.

It is easy to have keynoters come in or to make stimulating presentations, but the real impact of these sessions comes in the follow-through. Once you have piqued the interest of your staff, you will want to follow up with sessions that determine the implementation plan for your organization. That is exactly what the next sessions should accomplish. Remember, this is not to be just a cheer-leading session where you simply expose people to new ideas; rather, it should be a kickoff for a yearlong theme that will result in changes—visionary changes—for your organization. That will require continuous reinforcement on your part as well as continuous education.

Following the kickoff, I always provided time for internalization. This included formal and informal discussion of the ideas and changes. You will not want to rush this session, nor will you ever want to present ideas that you do not follow through on. A lack of follow through is a waste of everyone's time and the organization's money. In order to give credibility to the ideas presented these follow-up sessions should always be structured to include any keynote speakers who were involved in the earlier session. You will want to gather input in terms of potential goals, organizational measurements, or projects to be studied, but they should never just be discussion sessions with no end in mind. That end product, by the way, may end up being a decision not to pursue the topic under discussion; but again, that decision must be based on sound reasoning.

Because the first day was very global in nature—a stretch day, looking at the overall future directions of the organization—I always ended with some type of social event to develop camaraderie. The remaining days got into more specifics, always including a day spent reviewing the output data from the past year as well as the public input from the sessions conducted earlier. This is where I would expect the divisions to present

Step Five – Developing an Agile Leadership Team

their preliminary work on the planning process so that we could end the week with a laundry list of potential growth and retraction items for the next budget. The remaining days also included a combination of introductions to new topics and time for training sessions on the current topics that leadership staff were expected to be competent in.

Planning should always be a part of this session. It is your opportunity to infuse the outside information into the process and get people to begin looking at the big picture. I would spend at least one day with them, utilizing a trained facilitator to help them work through the initial skeleton of a plan for the next fiscal year. This might sound like a lot of lead time; but, trust me, once you start the academic year, the next budget year comes up quite rapidly, and any preparatory work is time well spent.

I believe that visionary leaders need to encourage continuous education. As a result, I always planned some training sessions as a part of this week and continued them throughout the year. These sessions, taught by instructors who knew the subject, were well laid out and included materials, competencies to be mastered, and testing. By the way, I always participated fully in these sessions, sometimes becoming the target of internal humor! Many of the training sessions were based on technology and on the utilization of data. As I stated previously, access to and the utilization of data is a key to visionary leadership, and so we necessarily spent time to create universal competence in that arena. External resources were often employed if it was determined that they were more on the cutting edge than internal staff. In all cases we invited other internal staff who had an interest in the topic to participate. Many times this led to enhanced curriculum being developed by our own faculty.

As the saying goes, I believe that you have to spend money to make money. That means you need to search out the best to train you if you want to be the best. You do not want to rely solely on internal or local talent simply because of cost or ease of access. To be the best, you must search out the best and pay the price of admission to that world. Staff expects you to lead, and you will need to do it in the best way possible.

Training usually occupied one or two days during the week and was also a part of each of the monthly sessions during the year. External talent was usually limited to the summer sessions or day-long sessions during the year, with the remaining sessions being handled by trained trainers who were on staff. I always looked to train our own staff as a part of any external contract we developed, because we needed follow-up and needed to train new staff on an ongoing basis.

The real test of a session like this was the feeling among participants that something positive had been accomplished. If I could not produce that feeling, the session had not met its goals. I would spend a great deal of preparation to ensure that would happen, perhaps even agonizing over the upcoming session too much at times. In the long run I developed a staff that was extremely competent and current in leading the organization, a state of affairs that was emphasized by their longevity at the organization. It was also emphasized by the fact that many were eventually promoted into higher-level positions, including my position when I retired. I support the concept that internal staff needs to be prepared to lead the organization into the future. Organizational development should not be interpreted to mean that you cannot or should not seek good candidates externally, because that is always important. Rather, organizational development creates a state of preparedness that allows your organization to flourish if better qualified external candidates are not available. I encouraged and participated in a number of programs to ensure that would occur.

Many leaders feel threatened by organizational development, fearing that others will be perceived as being better than they are. As a visionary leader, you need to be a champion for organizational development because that is the only way to give longevity and direction to your organization and to sustain the concepts that you have instilled. Therefore, the staff education programs I implemented at the college included internal, community, and state-level programs to foster organizational development. I will briefly step you through those that I utilized, giving reasons for each. I ensured that interested staff participated in each of the programs each year, and I selected participants on the basis of competition rather than simple application. I was constantly looking for future talent and seeking to encourage it. Criteria were established for each program, and only the most qualified applicants were selected. As a result, the programs were viewed as being important to the future of the college, and the candidates selected always received recognition both for being selected and for completing the program. It is critically important for you to consider completion of these programs as an important criterion in selection and promotion efforts. If you don't, they will all too soon be regarded by staff as being unnecessary or inconsequential. If, however, they are given status in the selection and promotion process, staff will see them as development tools for the future.

I will start at the state level and work down to the local level as I outline these programs. I was fortunate to head a task force for the college system in the middle 1990s to look at the future of leadership and devise a program to meet emerging leadership needs in our state. Previous programs had not been successful, and yet the need for new leaders was imminent because of anticipated retirements. As the task force began its work, they realized that the lack of success of previous programs was a result of several missing components. First of all, the previous programs had no defined competencies, no admission requirements, no method of evaluation, no consistency from year to year, and finally no recognition as a credential.

As this review continued, the new program began to take shape. Surveying senior leaders to determine the competencies needed for future leaders, the group utilized these competencies as the skeleton for a new program. It was discovered that past programs had given participants false expectations in that no admission requirements had been established. Thus people were allowed to participate who had no chance of moving into a leadership program because of lack of adequate education or experience to meet state certification requirements. The task force reviewed state certification requirements and set expectations for admission into the program to ensure that qualified candidates would be able to move into a leadership program at one of the state's colleges.

Having completed these two steps, a developer was sought to develop the curriculum and establish the credential. The state's college presidents reviewed the information and agreed to utilize the resulting program as an element in their hiring and promotion processes. The task force accepted a proposal submitted by the International Chair Academy located at Maricopa Community College in Arizona. The Chair Academy had its own program, including a mentorship, and they agreed to help develop the state program. As you might expect, what we needed and what they had already developed had some common elements, but due to state variations we needed some unique elements. A partnership ensued that resulted in a new state-level academy of the International Chair Academy. Their competencies, combined with a unique additional session and separate admission requirements, gave us what we needed. The resulting program, the Wisconsin Leadership Development Institute, began in 1995 and is still training future leaders for higher education in Wisconsin today. Many of the current college leaders in Wisconsin have come through this very successful academy. That program carries both state and national credentials. The national credential was a side benefit of the partnership, one which was considered important for candidates transferring out of the state.

An additional side benefit to participants is the granting of university credit for the program by several universities that view it as a significant entry to their own advanced degrees. Participants are now able to get a head start on an advanced degree in addition to obtaining a national credential. The program tuition is funded by the local colleges, which usually supply a minimum of two candidates annually. The significance of the program is emphasized by the attendance at the annual graduation ceremony of the college presidents and candidate mentors. I encouraged potential leaders at all levels to consider this program. Even seasoned veterans who came on staff in senior positions were expected to obtain the credential, which I felt gave them a sound basis to begin their evolution as visionary leaders. The mentorship program is especially critical, for it gives participants great access to personnel and events that they might not otherwise have.

Community involvement is a critical element of leadership in higher education, and I always encouraged all of my leadership staff and faculty to get involved in their communities and to participate in community leadership programs. Most chambers of commerce and some non-profit organizations support leadership programs. We annually placed people in these programs to learn about their community and to establish the relationships that would allow them to help those communities grow through mutual partnerships.

Finally, I also worked with senior leaders to develop an internal leadership development program targeted to staff who over time might be interested in leadership positions. This program had the least restrictive admission requirements and was designed to help people evaluate their potential for leadership, give them insight into the positions that are available, and finally help them to develop a professional development plan that would meet their goals should they decide that was what they wanted. Obviously, this program targeted younger, more inexperienced staff and was designed to help them and the organization plan for the future. The mixture of staff who participated in this program was interesting because it included faculty, clerical, and support staff who were considering changing direction. The resulting plans were supported by the college wherever possible because it helped to create the future of the organization.

This chapter has focused on leadership development, but I have covered only part of the picture. Leadership occurs at many levels in an organization. If you are to be considered visionary, then your ideas must permeate the organization. Many times faculty and support staff are your front-line people; and if they don't know what is going on, you are quickly going to be in quicksand or worse! I always set up sessions at least twice a year for these groups so they would have the information necessary to tell the story. Nothing is worse than to have someone ask a receptionist about a program and have the receptionist say, "I never heard about that!" As a leader I always told the story to these groups; and if a leadership training topic was appropriate, these individuals were encouraged to attend as well. Do not make the mistake of expecting others to tell your ideas to these groups. As a visionary leader, you know that each and every individual is critical to the overall implementation of where you want to go, and they need to hear it from you. The last thing you want is to have the staff of your organization feel they are not important. For that reason, specialized sessions to help them improve in their roles by better understanding the organization and its direction are critical.

I would be remiss if I did not address trustees. Their training is key as well. Obviously, they are busy people and can't be expected to spend large amounts of time; but I did annual retreats that including training and always made certain that the trustees were invited to any of our regularly scheduled staff-training sessions, especially to the kickoff of the summer session. Their level of training mirrored that of the staff, so the trustees knew and ultimately supported how the college operated. I also supported their attendance at their state and national organizations. Most importantly, I made sure that they were aware of the college's operational plan and vision.

In conclusion, I feel that all of these programs are critical in the development of an organization. As a visionary leader, you will need to consider them as you develop your own ideas and directions. You might be getting the feeling that your time is not your own as a visionary leader. There is some truth to that! The leader of any organization who is worth his or her salt will be involved, and that requires commitment and time. I don't have any easy answers on that one, other than to say that you have to always monitor your involvement and prioritize what is critical. If the job were easy, anyone could do it. As I was told many times, "That's why they pay you the big bucks."

Remember, an idea that cannot be actualized will never become a vision, and actualization can only be accomplished through others. You always need to go back to that first component of visionary leadership, which is determining what is of value to people. Once you do that, then you can never underestimate the power of education as you lead them toward that visionary goal.

Step Six –
Partnerships: The Glue for Your Visionary Plan

As a visionary, never worry about recognition.

Many times leaders worry too much about their own self worth and compromising their ideas. As a result, they avoid developing relationships with others to make a vision happen. I have found that concern to be a myth; many times just the opposite is true. Partnerships have been the cornerstone of my tenure in leadership over the years, partnerships that have paid off in spades in terms of the final outcomes that were made possible. Developing partnerships and sharing the outcomes and recognition must become the trademark of your visionary leadership. Others who may not be as forward thinking as you or who are not risk-takers will usually work very hard to help your vision become a reality, if it is truly a win-win situation. Therein is the key. As a visionary leader, you will need to work very hard to identify those elements of your vision that can be beneficial to a potential partner. I have brought partners into projects who had much more status than I did because they were able to recognize that partnering on a given project gave them some new recognition or capability.

As you look to partner, look for easily recognizable and concrete elements of benefit for all parties as opposed to long-term "maybes." I would rather err on being conservative in my promises to a potential partner and end up with more rather than betting the house and not producing the expected results. Similarly, as you look for partners, look outside of your normal venue to find those who might benefit but who would not be considered natural suitors. Remember, just because something has never been attempted doesn't mean it is not a great idea. Don't give up easily. Good partnerships are usually forged over time. I have found that the most difficult ones to develop are often the most rewarding. I have worked on partnerships that others told me were not possible, but because I was persistent and patient they eventually worked out. If you come to my city today, those partners will recognize the resulting projects as visionary moves that were truly win-win.

In this chapter, I would like to walk you through several of those so-called visionary projects and the corresponding partnerships that were necessary to make them a reality. These projects will help you to understand the use of partnerships. More importantly, they show how all six of the steps of visionary leadership fit together into a gestalt. You will also see that it is possible for you to become a visionary leader by following the steps we have discussed in this book. Let's take a closer look.

The Health Education Center

In the early '90s and continuing today, modeling and forecasting showed that the need for allied health and nursing graduates was going to sky rocket. My college had a number of programs in that arena, but the substantial medical sector in the region made me realize that more graduates and more programs would be needed. While adding programs sounded like a good plan, it had some roadblocks that needed to be overcome. Most allied health and nursing programs utilize internships at hospitals and clinics as a major training component, but those institutions can only accommodate a finite number of interns at any given time. The problem is further complicated by multiple organizations in a region that train health workers at various levels needing internship sites. Competing for the same training slots were public universities, community colleges, private institutions in the region, and institutions from outside of the region. The scope of the problem was enormous, but it was not a new

Step Six – Partnerships: The Glue for Your Visionary Plan

problem. For years I had encountered this roadblock as I attempted to change or grow health education programs. When I met with the leaders at the clinics and hospitals, I usually received positive overtures; but the positive responses usually were blocked somewhere between the top of the organization and the working units where the internship was to happen. I began to recognize the lack of internship sites as a situation where the college had potential for adding value. The resulting value in this case was threefold. First of all, the healthcare providers would find value in more graduates. Secondly, the college would find value in solving a long-standing problem. Most importantly, prospective students would be able to get training when and where they wanted it. The situation was truly of value to customers both internally and externally.

About the same time I began to look at a number of other seemingly unrelated developments. A division dean was doing research in the use of simulation in education as a part of her doctoral research. While this was a new area and virtually untested as an educational methodology, it was intriguing, albeit expensive. I encouraged her to investigate it as a potential solution to the ongoing bottleneck in health education. At the same time, I began to investigate the possibility of an on-campus clinic that could be used as a clinical site for students. Universities have such operations, but they have resident students as patients; even then the cost is many times subsidized. As a commuter technical college, we did not have a large on-campus population.

I had the opportunity to sit on the community advisory committee for a teaching family practice clinic in our community operated by the University of Wisconsin Medical School. This was a full-service clinic with a teaching faculty and full-time residents completing their family practice residency. They were in cramped, aging facilities on the other side of town and were anxious to expand their number of residents and patients. Obviously, funding was a problem for them as well. I began conversation with the director of the clinic about my idea for an on-campus clinic. The conversation did not go anywhere at first because it was not something that was common–a partnership between a medical school and a technical college. Then there was the need for funding to make it happen.

This chapter should probably be titled persistence and patience, because that is what it took. I began to discuss a potential project with community members and other healthcare providers in the community, and over the next months we began to flesh out the idea and develop a plan. I also asked the college's architectural firm to do some initial sketches of a working/learning clinic. I am a big believer that pictures and words add credibility to an idea. Over time, the idea began to arouse the interest of the community as a future possibility, but one that would be really difficult to achieve in a community with a population of less than 100,000. Persistence was working, except that I wanted the idea to become a reality now, while others considered it an idea. The problem of funding was always the deal breaker.

In another unrelated development, the college had established a dental hygienist program in the early '90s, and the dental community had always pushed for more graduates. Again the clinical experience required by accrediting bodies prevented that expansion. At the same time, the communities in the region were experiencing a lack of dental care opportunities for low-income and Medicaid-supported individuals due to the reimbursement rates in Wisconsin.

Marquette University, having the only dental school in Wisconsin, is always looking for residency and internships for their students. I had the opportunity to meet with the dean of the Marquette dental school to discuss our dental hygienist program and to discuss the possibility of a partnership between our programs to give our students more experience in working with practicing dentists. The college had a small laboratory where students worked on other students, and the college utilized the offices of local dentists on a time-available basis, usually during evening hours.

As a result of those discussions, I began to investigate the possibility of another on-campus clinic that would be self-supporting and would provide services for low-income and Medicaid patients. I envisioned the

Step Six – Partnerships: The Glue for Your Visionary Plan

clinic to be staffed by our students and by dental students and residents from Marquette University. As I discussed this with the dean of the dental college and with the community, I found that most people felt it was a great idea but that, because of funding, it was not a realistic possibility. Again I had the architects add to the potential plan. Patience and persistence!

If you want to be a visionary leader, you need to be willing to step up to the plate with an idea and take the risks necessary to sell it to others. I have always been amazed by the number of great ideas that never see the light of day because the idea goes contrary to what has always been done. An idea must be of value to the consumer, and in this case the solution to the multiple concerns of three organizations would be a win-win-win situation. Many ideas end at this point, but if you are to become a true visionary leader, you must develop the persistence and patience to continue on from there.

As the architects sketched a plan, they also attached a price tag to it—and of course it was startling! It was about twelve million dollars, and that included remodeling the existing health center and doubling that space to include a simulation center and two working clinics. Persistence and patience were really going to be necessary! I should give you a bit of information about our capital planning and budgeting at this time. The technical colleges in our state are not funded for capital improvements through the state. Rather, the plans are approved at the state level, and funding comes from the local tax base which in our case consists of eleven counties. Additionally, if more than one million dollars is needed, a referendum is required in all eleven counties. Now, I successfully conducted one successful referendum during my tenure to replace some out-of-date facilities in manufacturing and emergency services and build a new campus in a city at a distance from the central campus. While that referendum passed with sixty-eight percent of the vote, it was the only referendum ever conducted in the history of the college. To accomplish that, I personally made 125 presentations and had a lot of industry support to make that a reality. I say that not to impress you but rather to make the case that referendums are not something taken lightly. I knew that a health education center with working clinics would not be likely to pass a referendum.

The alternative was to raise the money through a capital campaign that would take it outside of the normal taxing bodies and give a lot more latitude. Yet in a region like the one the college is located in, this was an uphill battle because of the limited population and industrial base. As I worked with health industry leaders, my trustees, and my foundation board, we put together a plan that had several facets. That resulting plan included borrowing up to the legal limit of one million dollars, the remaining sum to be solicited from private donations, foundations, and the federal government. By that time I had stirred up considerable interest in the project, but as a realist I knew that most people believed it would not be possible and were sitting back to watch. You will find that most people will not venture their support to visionary projects until they see a reasonable chance of success, so don't be disillusioned by this seeming lack of support for your ideas. Persistence and patience will win them over as you proceed toward your goal.

I prepared a proposal and presentation to sell the project at the local, state, and federal levels. Since no model was available as a reference point, the job of convincing was even more difficult. Over a period of one year, the necessary funds were raised, with money provided by the federal government through several appropriations grants, a state-level advanced technology center grant, financial participation from all of the healthcare providers in the region, and donations from many private citizens and faculty. It was not easy, but even the doubting Thomases became believers. When we broke ground, I made certain that all of our partners were there, no matter how small or large, to take their bow and receive recognition for participating in a very unique, risky, and visionary project.

The project received national recognition, and in my estimation it exemplifies what is possible when the steps of visionary leadership are utilized. It was born out of need, and it added value to the many partners and our students. The resulting facility houses two working clinics, both

Step Six – Partnerships: The Glue for Your Visionary Plan

which serve as learning sites for students and as operational sites for community patients. The facility today houses seventeen programs, all with laboratories that could serve as a working hospital in the event of a major emergency. Laboratories from nursing wards to a functioning surgery center to radiography and sonography clinics make this center a true model for the future of health education. In addition, a unique center with three sophisticated human-patient simulators and a virtual hospital helps students in the programs get the practice time they need using simulation before they work on the real thing—you and me!

Perhaps the most intriguing parts of the facility are the clinics and the major partners, the University of Wisconsin Family Practice Clinic and the Marquette Dental School. The college now has a working dental clinic that serves low-income and Medicaid patients with students from Marquette University Dental School and the college's dental hygienist and dental assistant students. The clinic sees over three thousand patients annually and was financially in the black within three years. The University of Wisconsin Family Medicine Clinic provides the college's students with opportunities they would not have otherwise to work with physicians. There are fifteen resident family practice physicians located at the center, and they work with the college's radiology, ultrasound, clinical laboratory, and nursing students utilizing real patients and some of the most sophisticated equipment available. This is another situation that really has become a true win-win outcome. Obviously, there are always challenges in these types of situations; but left to their own capabilities, the staffs of all three organizations have learned to work as one and have taken the original thinking to a level I never thought possible in the beginning.

As I said, this center was born out of necessity. Because of that reason, it has added value to the partners, to the students being trained, and to the healthcare providers through an increased number of graduates. Through these clinics and through human-patient simulation, the college is able to give students more clinical training on-site. This advanced training results in better prepared students as they enter their clinical experience and allows the healthcare providers to absorb more students at any given time.

If you walk through the facility you will think you are in a major hospital, and you will be amazed by the simulation center. The part that impresses me most is the Wall of Fame. On this wall in the central commons is a listing of all of the partners who took a risk because it was of value to them. They made it a reality! A project like this exemplifies the steps in visionary leadership that were discussed in previous chapters. Value was determined by the customers. Some of them were internal customers (staff and students); others were external customers (regional healthcare providers); but all of them had a problem that could not be solved by traditional thinking. It involved taking risks and advancing an untried idea, and it resulted in bringing two major universities and a technical college together in a major medical training facility in a community of less than 100,000 people. Many doubted that it would ever be reality, and that was a key to knowing the project was on the cutting edge. From inception of the idea to ribbon cutting, communication was key among legislators, donors, healthcare providers, and the public. A business plan steeped in data was necessary to make it happen, and a great deal of informing and training of leadership staff was required. As you can see, it took time, but consistency and planning were the keys. People consider it visionary, but in the final analysis it was a well-executed process.

Now let's take a look at another project that was considered by many to be a visionary project and see how it followed the same steps we have been discussing. Again you will see that, while it was viewed by many as being visionary, it was really the result of utilizing the six steps of visionary leadership.

Nanotechnology Program and the NanoRite Innovation Center

I started thinking about nanotechnology in the early '90s when the governor of Wisconsin organized a manufacturing conference for the technical colleges and the state's manufacturing community. The manufacturers attending that conference told us that we had to help them become more productive and introduce them to new technologies

Step Six – Partnerships: The Glue for Your Visionary Plan

so they could remain competitive within the global market. This seemed relatively simple on the surface; but as I pondered the request, it provided a real challenge. The productivity part of the request was fairly easy, because the college had done a lot of curriculum and program development in that arena; but the new or advanced technologies request was more concerning. When asked about the technologies needed, we found very little response from the manufacturing community except that it had to impact their bottom line in a positive way. I knew then that I had encountered a problem that, if solved by the college, would add value to our customers. Obviously, the status quo was not acceptable. It was time to do some research and collect some data for analysis.

As a visionary leader, you always need to be on the lookout for solutions or clues to possible solutions. Later that year I attended a conference in Milwaukee, and a session attracted my attention. It was entitled "The Next Big Thing Is Really Small," and it was presented by Jack Uldrich, CEO of NanoVeritas, a consulting firm in the Twin Cities of Minnesota. The name of the session happened to be the title of a book he had written. As Jack outlined the impact of nanotechnology on the world as we know it, the lights went on for me. He outlined how nanotechnology was happening around the country and the world. He referred to it as a disruptive technology and predicted that it would have an impact bigger than that of the industrial revolution. Today nanotechnology is a relatively common term, but that was not the case in the early '90s, at least not with the general population.

This session piqued my interest, and I began to do more research on the topic. As a visionary leader you will need to cultivate the smallest seeds that you come across, even though many of those seeds will not bear fruit. This trait separates followers from leaders, for many times followers bypass critical items as being irrelevant, too futuristic, or too difficult to accomplish. I read the book and scoured the internet for more information. I called Jack and found he was willing to talk more about the subject. I also learned that the Twin Cities were a hotbed for applications of nanotechnology. Now the Twin Cities are a little over a hundred miles west of the college, and many economic development efforts crossed the state line. I discovered that much work in nanotechnology had been done by 3M Corporation, which had its headquarters there. I was able to get a meeting with their lead scientists; and when I described nanotechnology as an emerging technology (which it was for our state and certainly my college), they quickly informed me that they had been working with it for over thirty years. They were eager to provide information, encouragement, and support for the idea.

Visionary leadership data comes in many forms. In the early stages it is important for you to realize that information collected and verified from numerous sources is a key. Do not rely on data from one source, because it can take you in the wrong direction. Rather, you will need to collect your data and organize it in a manner that makes sense to you. A "white paper" is that type of instrument for me. It allows me to organize data and look at it from various angles. If I can build a solid case from the data, it makes sense to me to move on to the next stage. I find that writing helps me to visualize things more clearly, so I started to develop a "white paper" on the implementation of a nanotechnology program at the college. The program I envisioned would serve the region by getting a head start on the development of the economy. As I continued my research on nanotechnology and other advanced technologies, I began to organize the plan or vision in my mind and on paper. The more I learned and the more information I collected, the more convinced I became that nanotechnology would be a source of value to my customers.

The next stage involved communicating the thought process to others, especially to those who would be impacted by the decision. These are the individuals who have a problem or a concern and who need the solutions you are attempting to develop. If they see it as an adequate solution, you will have the potential for added value for them, and the solution can continue to evolve. My first step in carrying this potential solution to the next level was to introduce the topic to business leaders in the community. Having done my homework, I set the stage by releasing the white paper to various key groups. Again, as I pointed out earlier,

Step Six – Partnerships: The Glue for Your Visionary Plan

you need to track responses for consistency. That was especially critical in this case, when I was introducing a topic like nanotechnology to a medium-sized community and suggesting that it would be a solution for manufacturing in the region! The previous example of a health education center was a cakewalk in comparison!

As a visionary leader, you must develop and cultivate a reputation with your audiences. This does not just happen. Rather, it happens by design. By the time I got to this stage, I had accomplished several things that gave people the confidence I was able to make things happen. I had helped the college pass its only referendum in the eleven-county region which resulted in a new manufacturing education center in an industrial park, an emergency services education center, and a new regional campus. In addition, the new health education center had become a reality. Both of these projects had received a great deal of media exposure, because I made a point of keeping college news in front of people through a planned and organized process. Without that background, this proposed project might have been thought of as long shot or just an idea; but because of past successes it was taken seriously. Patience and persistence always pay off!

The next step was to set up a community forum sponsored by the college with Jack Uldrich as a keynoter! Remember, you can always bring in mentors or quasi-mentors who support your idea, but make certain they are charismatic speakers who can captivate an audience and help to promote the value of your idea. Jack Uldrich filled that bill. He was very knowledgeable and credentialed, and had the knack of taking a very complex subject and making it understandable to the layman. Of course, we invited the press and made provisions for them to have a separate audience with the speaker. As a result of that presentation and the white papers, several key community leaders came on board with the idea, and the project was off and running.

Another community college in Minnesota had begun to research a similar program, so I contacted them to see if they were interested in a partnership. They were, and thus a two-state partnership was born that gave even more credibility to this new direction. Remember that credit is not important in visionary leadership. Many times partnerships can make things happen that would not otherwise be possible. Another similar partnership evolved with the two-senior level universities in the region because of their curricula in materials science and technology. I contacted them and began to work with their scientists on the idea of pooling resources to develop a regional approach to nanotechnology that would produce two-year and four-year graduates, thereby making an even greater impact on the region. It is well known that community of interest is critical to the economic development of a region. Richard Florida in his book *The Rise of the Creative Class* discusses this concept. Communities that attract and keep young, well-educated graduates do so by providing opportunities for them to associate and share ideas with other individuals having the same vocation or a similar educational background. If the region served by the college was to attract and keep graduates in the nanosciences, it became obvious that we had to provide these types of "think tank" opportunities. By partnering with the other higher education organizations and bringing in the business community, we would not only produce more graduates but also provide opportunities for new graduates to associate with other practicing professionals in the region.

As a result, the curriculum was developed and a two-year degree in nano-science technology was born as a partnership involving two community colleges, two universities, and the support of the manufacturing community. The interest and excitement in the community had ratcheted up to a new level. The manufacturing community began to look to the educational institutions for leadership in this new technology, valuing the presence of knowledgeable faculty as well as access to equipment made available through these programs.

Visionary leaders need to always be looking for the next step and the next value-added solution. They can never rest on their past successes. The idea that the manufacturing community was interested in the equipment and expertise of the educational institutions began to intrigue

Step Six – Partnerships: The Glue for Your Visionary Plan

me. Major research universities have developed partnerships with the business community for decades. Why, I wondered, could we not use that model by combining several universities and a technical college on a smaller scale? I began my research by making contact with the University of Wisconsin Research Park and the Wisconsin Technology Council. The individuals who run those organizations had a great deal of experience in this arena and could again act as my quasi-mentors. From those discussions and from discussion with community leaders, the idea of an innovation center for nanotechnology was born. The information that I had collected was again organized into a white paper so as to really ensure that the direction was legitimate and that, while risky, it had potential for success.

Remember that this type of project was not necessarily a conventional educational mission; it was certainly not a community-college mission. It would have to have community support, college trustee support, staff support, and state approval even before financing was considered! It would require a great deal of sound data along with a substantial public relations campaign to become reality. The white paper was refined and circulated for review among a small group of insiders to ensure that it made sense. That paper proposed an innovation center operated by the college that would provide space for applied research by businesses interested in new products or processes involving nanotechnology. The center would provide start-up space for new industries in the nanotechnology arena and access to college and university faculty and equipment. It would also house some expensive clean-room space. My research had shown that start-up businesses and industries working on new products needed this type of space, expertise, and equipment to do their developmental work. In fact, many of them preferred an ongoing relationship with higher education because of the cutting-edge work they were involved in.

From the white paper, a business plan evolved, because good ideas remain just that unless, as a visionary leader, you can find ways to finance them and show the necessary outcomes. Along with a business plan, I asked the architects to develop rudimentary plans for a NanoRite

Innovation Center. A picture is worth a thousand words, and when combined with a beginning business plan, it could answer the questions that boards and financing groups might have for a "visionary" or risky project. I emphasize the word "visionary" once more because, as you have seen, NanoRite was the result of the process that has been outlined in the book. It was not just a vision that came to me one day. With patience and persistence, the same process can work for you.

The plan was eventually approved by the community, trustees, and the state. Then the quest for financing began. This is where it becomes lonely as a visionary leader. Don't expect everyone to rally around you as you move toward making a plan reality. Usually it results in people sitting back to see if you can make the idea work. That is usually the point where you know you are on the cutting-edge—or, as some say, the "bleeding edge." This is why the research and data phase is so critical. As a visionary leader, you need to know that the risk is both possible and worth the effort, because you will have to go it alone for a period of time.

To keep everyone aware of the project and the progress, it is critical to utilize your public relation skills during this stage. Even if the going is slow, the worst thing you can do is to be silent. Regular media releases were utilized, reports were given to the appropriate boards and groups, and community forums on related topics were held to keep the interest up. As a visionary leader, you must become the cheerleader and utilize your best skills to ensure that the belief in the vision is maintained and that any skepticism is turned around. There will always be naysayers. As a visionary leader, you need to keep them informed as well and not turn your back from them. They can be an important gauge for you. If more are moving away from your idea than toward it, you may want to evaluate the reasons.

The economy of the region is always of concern to many, and I utilized that to garner support. In the long run, I was able to put together local, state, and federal financing to build the facility. The real key was gaining the support of local and regional industries as well as local government. Their support showed that they believed in the project.

Step Six – Partnerships: The Glue for Your Visionary Plan

The industries included not just major industries but also some smaller, vibrant industries that were willing to become investors, even tenants in the building, so they could evolve in new directions.

Today NanoRite is nearing capacity and stands as a symbol of progress for the region. The progress is slow but evolving. As the medical-device industry became a target sector for the region, a micro-manufacturing curriculum and center evolved. A Class 100 cleanroom houses key equipment used not only by students but also by the industries in the region. New industries have located in the industrial park surrounding the college because of relationships that they view as win-win.

As this project and the health education center became reality, I always emphasized the partners in rather elaborate ribbon-cutting ceremonies that lasted longer than perhaps they should have. The credit went to the partners, because without them any visionary plan is just that–a plan. Don't ever worry about your credit, because that is not what makes you a visionary leader. Getting things accomplished that others thought impossible is what it is all about.

These two projects tell the story of visionary leadership, and that is why I have used them as examples. They emphasize all of the steps outlined in this book and show that visionaries are not born. Visionary leadership is the result of determining what is of value to customers, doing research and collecting data, taking risks, planning, communicating effectively, being persistent, exercising patience, and following through. Visionary leadership does not happen overnight; but by utilizing the steps outlined in this book, you can achieve things that others consider visionary.

Conclusion – The Personal Traits of a Visionary

Everything you need to know you learned in high school.

As I have stated many times throughout this book, confidence is not something visionary leaders are born with. It is something they learn and develop by using the right tools. Some of those tools are very, very basic; others are more complex. I often tell people that the three most valuable courses I took in high school were algebra, speech, and typing. In my estimation, these courses were foundational, though I did not recognize them as such at the time, for they helped me develop skills that I used throughout my career as a leader. When I was a student in high school, who knew that the personal computer would become the major communication link that it is today? And what is critical for using that tool? Typing skills, of course!

My study of algebra has also been a foundation stone. With a working knowledge of basic algebra comes the ability to analyze data and help to predict the future. I often wonder how many times I have run a basic algebraic formula with one unknown to analyze a situation and determine the best course of action; algorithms, too, can be utilized to help create consistency and objectivity. Data analysis is a critical tool for research, and both algorithms and analysis are essential in determining the best course of action and reviewing the outcomes.

For visionary leaders, however, public speaking skills are by far the most critical tool. You can have access to all the necessary data and be the best analyzer in the world, but if you don't have the charisma and speaking skills to sell your idea and convince people that you are to be trusted and followed, then all is lost. Think of the speaking skills and the charisma that the great visionary leaders of our time possessed—leaders such as John F. Kennedy, Martin Luther King, Ronald Reagan, and William Jefferson Clinton, and, most recently, Barack Obama. They all used their speaking skills and charisma to lead us in new directions. Maybe they were individually not that great, but their skills in delivering their message captivated us, motivated us, and moved us in directions we had not thought possible.

I will always remember the selection process I went through in becoming a college president. It was grueling, and it included many "opportunities" to speak extemporaneously and be questioned before various audiences. At the time I questioned the logic of so many different situations; but after serving in that leadership position for years, I understood that this was the selection committee's way of evaluating a candidate's leadership style and, more importantly, his skills.

My advice to you, then, is to hone these necessary skills to perfection. If you are uncomfortable in any of these arenas, you must do as my daughters tell me: "Deal with it." These skills are foundational. The good news is that resources are available to help you develop or improve the skills of data analysis, public speaking, and technology utilization. Deal with them until they are invisible to you, and this will give you the all important tool of confidence.

Now let's move on from these basic or foundational skills to other personal skills for building your confidence as a visionary leader. That takes us to communication. Communication seems to be an elusive issue of constant concern for leaders, so I would suggest that you learn to understand and deal with it as soon as possible. Every evaluation by accrediting bodies deals with communication, and most organizations run climate surveys to determine the status of communication in the organization. Leaders often tell me that they communicate through emails, newsletters, in-service programs, and other meetings, and yet these same leaders sometimes get low marks on communication from their staff and communities.

Communication is integral to visionary leadership because it is the personal skill that allows you to integrate all six of the steps to leadership that we have discussed. You may be able to utilize your skills for determining value, validating data, evaluating risks, and developing partnerships; but unless you are able to communicate your goals to others, you will never complete the cycle and lead the organization. Communication, however, is not just being able to state your plan; it means believing in your plan, being able to discuss the plan in detail, giving solid reasons and data to support the direction or plan—and doing that over and over clearly and concisely until people understand and are willing to follow. Successful communication does not mean that everyone will agree with you. Rather, it means that they will understand where you are directing them, trust in you, and be willing to work with you. To accomplish that level of trust, you must be constantly observe their reactions and make necessary adjustments. As a result, organizational communication and the corresponding plan is not something you can delegate. Staff, community members, and the press assume that you, the visionary leader, are the one responsible for communication, and they are right.

Every year as I prepared our budget I would hold town hall meetings in various locations throughout our region. These sessions were established to gather input on our plan, listen to concerns, and explain the direction of the college. As president of the college, I led each of those sessions. People expect their leaders to do that; and when you do not appear, problems begin to occur. Because of heavy schedules, it is sometimes tempting to let someone else handle it, but I maintain that your personal involvement in these sessions is a "must."

Good media relations are another "must." As a visionary leader, you are the person whom the media expects to be in the know. You are the one they will contact. Good communication as a leader means that you will not put them off but will be willing to answer any questions (except, of course, those that you cannot answer for legal reasons). I always gave the media direct access to me and made it a point to get back to them quickly even if I was out of the office. That paid off in spades in several ways. First of all, they learned to trust me; and when I was not able to answer their questions because of legal concerns, they respected my wishes. Second, when I wanted to get something out for public relations purposes, they usually accommodated. I also met with each media outlet at least once a year to lay out future plans and allow them to ask questions. These courtesies also paid dividends when I needed their help in getting the word out on a topic.

As a visionary leader, you can never communicate too much. I sometimes used the statement, "Wherever there are two or more people gathered together, I am ready to tell the story of the college." That is how frequently you must communicate. I like to tell a story about communication with the community. My public relations manager came to me with the idea that I should do a television show about the college on our community public-access channel. My first reaction was that this was a waste of time because no one really paid attention to that channel. Well, he was persistent, and I finally agreed to give it a try for a couple of months. We put together a half-hour show that was broadcast several times each week during the month, and then we would tape another. I don't like scripted sessions because they seem too rigid, so we devised a program in which I would interview someone from the college on a current topic. Each segment of the show was twelve minutes, and we did two segments in a half-hour period, along with an introduction by me and some advertising about the college. To emphasize the role of the college in the communities we served we called the program "Reach for Success."

The results were interesting. Community people seeing me in a social setting or even in a retail store would approach me and say, "I watched you on TV," or, "You're the guy on TV talking about the college." And they could always relate something we discussed! We surmised that something must have caught their attention as they were channel surfing, prompting them to stop and watch for a few minutes. As a result, we utilized this means of communication with the community for many years. I use this story to emphasize that communication happens in many ways. It is a critical part of your job as visionary leader. Communication must be constant, and it must involve you as a key leader in your organization. If you want to lead with vision, you must hone these skills to perfection. Your plan will not succeed unless it is communicated properly.

You need to be visible and accessible because as a visionary leader you are the one that is setting the overall direction for the organization, and people want to hear it—from you. This does not mean you have to be a micro-manager, but you need to show that you are committed to the direction you have set. When Apple Computer unveils a new product, who is center stage? Steven Jobs, of course! And we have confidence in him as a visionary leader. He has proven himself, and we believe in him. Even in spite of formidable personal health problems he was there. If you are truly to be a visionary leader, you must accept that role. As you do so, the public will believe in your organization and believe that you can make a difference.

You will need to get used to public relations because you will be in the spotlight on almost a daily basis, whether you are meeting with editorial boards, developing paid commercials, or being accessible to the press. Get used to it. It goes with the territory. Good visionary leaders enjoy that role, are comfortable with it, and become good at it. Nothing will kill your momentum faster than avoiding the public relations role.

You will also need broad shoulders to handle difficult questions and points. The best advice for a visionary leader is not to avoid hard questions or challenging adversaries. Instead, tackle them head on and honestly. In today's environment, everyone from the media to the community to your students is more assertive than ever before. If you are not straight with them, they will find out quite quickly, and that will be much more uncomfortable for you than being up front.

As usual, it is the little things that count! A visionary leader needs to be with customers regularly, and that means paying attention to many things that we sometimes don't consider as important. For example, I always kept a box of note cards at my desk and would send handwritten notes (not emails) to people for a variety of things, from promotions to illnesses. I made a point of thanking everyone for help at an event or for including me. Visionary leaders need to know what is of value to the people around them, and they do this by staying in touch with them and their lives. If people view you as human because you send handwritten notes, tell amusing anecdotes about yourself, or admit that you "screwed up," they will be more comfortable as you work with them in the future. Your personal side as a visionary leader is important because you want to be approachable and accessible. For example, I always maintained an open-door policy with staff and the public. Believe me, that was difficult at times, but I knew I needed to spend time when people did come to me even though I might be staring at a desk full of work. The words must not be hollow. You will need to practice what you preach, or you will be found out quite quickly.

As a visionary leader, you need to take criticism without killing the messenger. It is easy to become so confident in your ideas that criticism is difficult to accept. Anger is not the answer, although that does not mean you should not defend your ideas. When we were building the health education center that I discussed in the last chapter, for example, such an event occurred. In order to make room for the new center we had to relocate a popular daycare center that had been in existence for some time. That center had lost money for years, however, and we had developed alternate plans that made great sense to me and solved a number of problems, not the least of which was money. Others did not see it that way, however! Well, I organized a public forum and invited the press to discuss the matter. Prior to opening the forum for discussion, I gave a presentation on the reasons. The open forum turned into a blistering hour. At least fifty people told me why it was a bad idea. Remember, I stated that I believe it is important for a visionary leader to confront his adversaries. No matter how difficult it was and no matter how unwilling people were to listen to the explanation, I knew I needed to be calm, attentive and, above all, not lose my temper.

While many affected by the idea were resistant, the media covered the event well, even though the headline was not particularly flattering. As you will learn if you haven't already, you cannot control the media! After the session we re-evaluated the entire concept to see if we had not done all of our homework, and we found it still made sense. Interestingly, one of our partners in the health education center stepped forward and made an offer. They allowed our students and instructional programs to utilize their daycare center and offered an enhanced partnership that became a win-win situation for all.

Because I didn't lose my cool, people appreciated the situation even more. It is true that staff and community like to see their leaders squirm at times, but I believe it is to see what they are really made of and not out of contempt. If you are going to be a visionary leader, then you have to understand that intense public scrutiny goes with the territory. At times you will need to change your well-laid plans, because the discovery of new data will change things. Don't ever become so vested in a plan that you will run with it in spite of what you are being told. I have seen many good leaders go down because they were unwilling to change or say they were wrong.

The interesting thing about visionary leadership is that you have to be prepared to deal with the idea that "perception is reality" to the people you are working with. Many times I was amazed to hear interpretations of things that I had said. My first reaction was, "That is not what I said," or, "That is not what was meant by what I said." What you, as a visionary leader, are dealing with is "perception," not "reality"—so be prepared! I often thought it would be interesting to send out an email announcing a fictitious change and then watch the flow of information that followed.

This leads me to another point concerning the reality of visionary leadership, and that is that what you say can and will be held against you. I tend to think out loud, meaning that I verbalize my thoughts publicly. I found out quite quickly that I needed to change this practice because as a leader, and especially as change agent, people would hang on my every word. What I said quite quickly became the law or reality of the land. I learned to temper that habit because I found myself refuting the response days later, explaining that I was considering an action as a possibility, not as a certainty. Usually, however, the rumor mill was already grinding away. I also learned rapidly to write emails very sparingly and then to read, reread, and reread them again before sending them out. If possible, I used the 24-hour rule concerning composing and sending out. What you will discover about your thought process in that time period will amaze you! I also learned never to respond with an email to something that upset me no matter how tempted I might be to do so. Emails are forever, and for many years to come they will come back to haunt you when you least expect them. In fact, as a leader I utilized all public electronic media very minimally. To avoid any surprises down the road, most of my composing and storage was done on my home computer.

Yes, there is, and always will be, a rumor mill. As a visionary leader, you might as well get used to it. Rumor mills exist in all organizations; and with the advent of electronic communication systems, those informal mills have been enhanced one hundredfold. It is fruitless to try and change or eliminate them. It is more profitable to recognize their existence. Be aware of what they are saying and use them to your advantage. Usually, people who are close to you will help by filling you in on what is going around. Rumor mills can actually help you, as a visionary leader, to determine what is of value to your customers. However, you need to be astute enough to sift fact from fiction, because some of the information in rumor mills is just idle gossip or worse, put there to create dissonance. Again, electronic communication has made it easy to circulate negative information while allowing anonymity for the author. My final word of advice to you, as a visionary leader, is to always be aware of your surroundings, electronic or otherwise. Change is a strange animal, and there are many people you will be working with who fear change. They fear it because it might cost them their position, their job, or just interrupt

Conclusion – The Personal Traits of a Visionary

their zone of comfort. Remember, just because you like or accept change as a way of life, many do not.

When I first became president, the college I was leading had been static for a long period of time. Staff was very comfortable with the status quo and embraced it even though our customers did not. I made some major changes early on that disrupted the status quo for staff, and it was amazing how quickly the "fear" word was evoked. The rumor mill was at its best, telling people to fear for their job and not to talk against the new president's plan or their job would be in jeopardy. It was impossible to learn where those fears came from, but they were there. I held many public forums to confront the topic head on and outlined, in fact, how far from the truth it really was. Eventually, the fear topic subsided. But rest assured that there are always those who resist change, who fear change, and who are willing to do anything to prevent it.

As a change agent, you will need an inner circle. To me an inner circle consists of one or two people who are your confidants. They are close staff members with whom you can think out loud and discuss your reasoning without having that information become public. They are also the people who will help you to keep abreast of organizational rumors and other information. Be very selective of the people you choose for your inner circle. They need to understand and believe in your direction, but they should not be "yes" people. They need to be the type of people who will look you in the eye and say, "That is the dumbest idea I have ever heard." And you need to be confident enough to take it to heart. These are people that you can use to flesh out ideas through give-and-take discussions, and they are the staff who can critique early versions of white papers, staff emails, or media releases.

Many times, these individuals are not line staff in the organization, and that is acceptable. It may cause some problems with your line staff, who think that the inner circle has too much access to you; but by being aware of this, you can usually handle the situation. Sometimes you are fortunate enough to have vice presidents who can play that role, but it doesn't always turn out that way. Again, be very cautious as a visionary leader if you move in the direction of an inner circle. You will find that a lot of people want to be in the inner circle, but few qualify. These are not positions that maintain a job description with clearly outlined duties; rather, these are individuals in whom you have confidence enough to confide your thinking and know it will not go any further.

Many times a president or chief executive officer will have a public relations specialist or special assistant who can serve as a member of that inner circle. I always had the person handle a number of different duties, including media releases, the organization of important special events such as legislative visits, and the review of my mail and correspondence when I was away from the office. This person always knew how to get in contact with me if something happened that required my immediate attention. That meant we were usually never away from the office at the same time.

You may be getting the idea that visionary leadership is a 24-7 proposition. I would not dissuade you from that thinking; successful visionary leaders are both involved and accessible. So what does that mean for you? Does it mean the end to life as you now know it? Probably not, because if you are reading this book, you already possess many of the characteristics that I have discussed in this book; you just have not put them together as we have been discussing. As a leader, I always took all of my vacation for we all know keeping a balance in life is important. Plans sometimes changed at the last minute, due to one situation or the other; but when that happened, I would simply re-schedule my down time.

When I was out of the office, and even when I was on vacation, I kept in touch with my office via email and voice mail early every morning but I would limit the time to a brief half hour. While this is a personal thing for each of you to decide, I always felt it was easier to keep running tabs for a half hour each morning than to face the deluge when I returned. Each of you is different and you have different family situations, so you will need to decide for yourself. One thing I emphasized to my staff, however, was that I did not value unused vacation as a positive part of their evaluation. Some people will try to impress you by the amount of

Conclusion – The Personal Traits of a Visionary

unused vacation that they have; and my response is that they were poor planners. We all need to keep healthy, physically and mentally or we will never become visionary leaders.

Visionary leadership is not about awards or rewards, nor is it about impressing others. Visionary leadership, in my estimation, is about getting the job done and getting it done right. It is about leading our economy, no matter which sector, into the future so that we create a better place to live, work, learn, and do business. If you are doing it for any other reason, you will be disappointed. Yes, you will be in the limelight perhaps more than you care to think about at times, but that is not what it is all about. I have seen too many leaders become disillusioned or disappointed because they didn't get the accolades they felt they deserved. We must always remember that any value we add is because we have made the world a better place in which to live. On my desk is a poem that I look at very often and, in fact, have recited to many graduates at commencement time. It is titled "What is Success" by Ralph Waldo Emerson, and it goes like this:

> To laugh often and much;
> To win the respect of intelligent people
> and the affection of children;
> To earn the appreciation of honest critics and
> endure the betrayal of false friends;
> To appreciate beauty;
> To find the best in others;
> To leave the world a bit better, whether by
> a healthy child, a garden patch or a redeemed
> social condition;
> To know even one life has breathed easier
> because you have lived;
> This is to have succeeded.

Those, my friends and colleagues, are the rewards are for visionary leadership. While you may view them as trite, you will know that they have come about only because you dared to take risks–calculated risks—to add value to the lives of others. Although good times mask poor leadership, during the years we are in and will be facing, visionary leaders will earn their place. Hopefully, you will be counted among them. Good luck as you use your new Crystal Ball!

About the Author

Bill Ihlenfeldt spent forty-two years in higher-education leadership working to change the face of the nations' community colleges. During his tenure he challenged higher education to operate utilizing a data-rich model designed to increase productivity and innovation and at the same time reduce costs. Utilizing those concepts in his leadership role,  which has been referred to as visionary, he led many innovative changes at the college. Those changes included incorporating simulation into healthcare education to increase the number and quality of graduates, a working on-campus health education center/clinic in partnership with a medical and a dental college, one of the nation's first nanotechnology programs, and a nanotechnology innovation center called Nano Rite to stimulate private sector economic development.

Ihlenfeldt modeled concepts like speed-to-market, risk, measurement-based outcomes, and algorithm-based modeling as a way of life during his career. These techniques, more common in the business world, were integrated into higher education resulting in a college that has received local, state and national recognition as a visionary college that has propelled the surrounding region and higher education into the 21st century.

Ihlenfeldt lives in Eau Claire, Wisconsin, with his wife Barbara.